POST KEYNESIAN
MONETARY ECONOMICS

POST KEYNESIAN
MONETARY ECONOMICS

Stephen Rousseas

M. E. Sharpe INC.
ARMONK, NEW YORK

Library of Congress Cataloging in Publication Data

Rousseas, Stephen William.
    Post Keynesian monetary economics.

    Bibliography: p.
    1. Monetary policy—History. 2. Keynesian economics. 3. Chicago
school of economics. I. Title.
HG230.3.R68   1986   332.4′6   85-14181
ISBN 0-87332-355-6
ISBN 0-87332-356-4 (pbk.)

Printed in the United States of America

To
Sidney Weintraub

Contents

Preface

Post Keynesian monetary economics is far from settled. This book is a critical overview of some of its central themes. It bears keeping in mind, however, that modern monetary policy can be said to have started four years after the March 1951 Treasury–Federal Reserve Accord—during the 1955–57 expansion when discretionary open market operations were first applied as the main tool of monetary policy. It is a bit difficult to believe that monetary policy, as we know it today, has been around for only thirty years, but it is so and this sober fact should be kept clearly in mind.

During this brief time the two major schools of monetary policy were the neoclassical Keynesians with their IS-LM models of fine-tuning, and the monetarists who started their rapid climb to dominance in the 1960s. Post Keynesian monetary economics rejects both of these approaches and it does so largely by reversing the causal arrow of the quantity theory of money. The money supply is seen as a function of nominal income rather than the other way around. What this amounts to is an *endogenous* theory of the money supply. More accurately, Post Keynesian monetary theory focuses on the *flow of credit-money* from the banking system to the business sector of the economy; or, alternatively stated, the causal arrow is, contrary to the usual textbook formulation, from the asset to the liabilities side of the banking industry's balance sheet. As will be argued in the text, this is more in keeping with Keynes's *Treatise* than with the *General Theory*'s portfolio-asset approach of liquidity preference theory.

If there is a leitmotif in this study, it is that the problem of financial innovations has been largely ignored by Post Keynesians. It needs to be incorporated into the theory of an endogenous money supply. Chapter 5 attempts to do so. And if this book can be said to have one single point of view, it is that an incomes policy by itself cannot be made to work without, at the same time, recourse to selective credit controls. This is a conclusion reached in Chapter 6, to which all the preceding chapters point, inexorably. Without doubt, that and other parts of this book will be found controversial and idiosyncratic, and not all those who call themselves Post Keynesians will be in full agreement. That, however, is to be expected in a field that is still struggling to find itself.

In a modest way, it is hoped that this study will at least bring some of the disagreements into the open and thereby prevent the emergence of what can only, in the nature of things, be an absurdity—"mainstream" Post Keynesian economics.

I am particularly indebted to Nancy J. Wulwick of LeMoyne College for her meticulous reading of the manuscript and for her many valuable suggestions, and to my students at Vassar College who patiently put up with the constant revisions of earlier versions of the manuscript.

Cap Ferret   SWR
August 1985

POST KEYNESIAN
MONETARY
ECONOMICS

CHAPTER 1

Introduction

The rise of neoclassical Keynesianism

Revolutions have a nasty way of devouring their progenitors and replacing them by a lesser and more arrogant breed who, in the name of the revolution, seek to consolidate its gains only to betray it in the process. The Keynesian revolution, in the realm of ideas, is a case in point, though in this instance the creator of the revolution was not quite the revolutionary others had made him out to be. Keynes himself, according to Joan Robinson, did not grasp the full import of his *General Theory*, and shortly after its publication in 1936 there were many heated discussions between him and his followers over what the *General Theory* "really" meant. The fact is that Keynes had never fully broken with his neoclassical upbringing at Cambridge under the tutelage of Alfred Marshall. His neoclassical heritage showed clearly in the opening pages of his *General Theory*. Though he rejected "Postulate II" of neoclassical theory, namely, that the supply of labor depends positively on the real wage, he did not openly reject "Postulate I," that the *demand* for labor is inversely related to the level of real wages. This half-way break with neoclassicism was to generate a great deal of mischief.[1] Still, his rejection of the neoclassical view that all unemployment was voluntary was, itself, a major breakthrough. Indeed, the notion of *involuntary* unemployment was the foundation of his revolution. Nevertheless, by downplaying the caveats attached to the end of each postulate concerning the existence of market power, it was possible for later neoclassical Keynesians to argue that Keynes accepted Postulate I and thus went along with the neoclassical idea that all firms are faced with increasing cost curves, the obvious counterpart of falling marginal productivity curves in a perfectly competitive market economy. This carry-over from neoclassical theory made the bowdler-ization of Keynes that much easier.

In the post–World War II period it is this "bastardized" version of Keynesian economics that has come to dominate economic thought. It is far to the right of the more traditional and earlier postwar Keynesian model that allowed for a less-than-full-employment equilibrium to exist, albeit one supposedly capable of being offset by an optimal combination of monetary and fiscal policy. Within the more extreme general equilibrium model of Keynes, distribution became an aspect of pricing in a free market economy operating under the "laws" of supply and demand. It was a return to a pre-Keynesian world of simultaneous equations and instantly adjusting markets. The economy once again is seen to tend naturally towards a full-employment equilibrium with the "laws" of marginal productivity analysis determining the distribution of income between capital and labor, i.e., *from each according to his ability, to each according to his contribution.* The distribution of the social product is thus legitimated by the impartial "laws" of econom-ics. What *is* is just; and any attempt to tamper with what *is* by unions, by government, or by big business serves only to make matters worse.

Convenient, self-serving conclusions followed easily. Any attempt by labor to achieve a larger slice of the pie than the market is prepared to allocate to it is bound to have an adverse effect on profits and thus on the rate of capital accumulation. The growth rate of the economy would fall as a result and the system would no longer be able to depoliticize the distribution of income through increases in the absolute level of well-being that growth makes possible. Capitalism would therefore quickly find itself in the throes of a serious legitimation crisis. In short, the viability of capitalism depends on continuous growth, which, in turn, depends on an unequal distribution of real output between capital and labor and labor's acquiescence in this seemingly unjust distribu-tion.

Keynes's early views on the distribution of wealth

In 1920, Keynes was in full agreement: "What an extraordinary epi-sode in the economic progress of man that age was which came to an end in August 1914! The greater part of the population, it is true, worked hard and lived at a low standard of comfort, yet were to all appearances, reasonably contented with this lot."[2] It was in "this economic Eldorado, in this economic Utopia" that Keynes and his contemporaries were brought up. "The projects and politics of militarism and imperialism, of racial and cultural rivalries, of monopolies, restrictions, and exclusion, which were to play the serpent to this paradise," wrote Keynes, "were little more than the amusements of . . . daily newspaper[s], and appeared to exercise almost no influence at all on the ordinary course of social and economic life."

The "psychology of society" was such as to organize itself socially and economically so as "to secure the maximum accumulation of capital." But while the daily conditions of life continued to improve for the mass of the population, "Society was so framed as to throw a great part of the increased income into the control of the class least likely to consume it." It was "the power of investment" and the economic growth that flows from it, not the "pleasures of immediate consumption," that was the driving force of a capitalism predicated on a maldistribution of wealth. In pre-capitalist society the aristocracy squandered its wealth on mansions, luxury goods, and frivolous baubles, which added nothing to the productive capacity of the economy. Stasis was the rule, not growth. It was only under capitalism and the Puritan ethic that the ruling class, the bourgeoisie, restrained its consumption in order to accumulate real capital. According to this argument, an equitable distribution of wealth would have precluded the "immense accumulations of fixed capital" that so greatly benefited all of mankind in the fifty years preceding the Great War. Indeed, as Keynes argued, "it was precisely the *inequality* of the distribution of wealth which made possible those vast accumulations of fixed wealth and capital improvements which distinguished that age from all others. Herein lay, in fact, the main justification of the Capitalist System." And this extraordinary achievement was predicated on the capitalist class's abstinence from consumption, which provided the savings out of which the accumulation of capital was financed. It was the capitalists who deserved most of the credit for the enormous increase in social welfare, not labor. Labor's main contribution was to go along, passively, with the unequal distribution of wealth which made it all possible; it was in its own best interest to do so. As Keynes put it:

> Thus this remarkable system depended for its growth on a double bluff or deception. On the one hand the classes accepted from ignorance or powerlessness, or were compelled, persuaded or cajoled by custom, convention, authority, and the well-established order of Society into accepting, a situation in which they could call their own very little of the cake that they and Nature and the capitalists were co-operating to produce. And

on the other hand the capitalist classes were allowed to call the best part of the cake theirs and were theoretically free to consume it, on the tacit underlying condition that they consumed very little of it in practice. The duty of ''saving'' became nine-tenths of virtue and the growth of the cake the object of true religion . . . And so the cake increased; *but to what end was not clearly contemplated.*

A gross inequality in the distribution of wealth and the incomes which flow from its private ownership were, for Keynes, ''a vital part of the pre-war order of Society and of progress as we then understood it.'' But this progress, as Keynes was well aware, depended on labor's passive and compliant willingness to go along. Nevertheless, ''It was not natural for a population, of whom so few enjoyed the comforts of life, to accumulate so hugely.'' And what Keynes most feared was that the laboring class would call the bluff and seek to appropriate for itself a larger part of the social pie at the expense of capitalist profits. In the resulting social upheaval, and as a prelude to a revolutionary restructuring of society, the capitalist class would then lose confidence in the future and ''seek to enjoy more fully their liberties of consumption so long as they last, and thus precipitate the hour of their confiscation.'' With the capitalist class no longer willing to save, accumulation would no longer be possible and the struggle over the distribution of income between capital and labor would become more and more intense leading ultimately to open class warfare and the demise of the capitalist system and all the benefits that derived from its earlier existence.

The distribution of wealth in the *General Theory*

This is where matters stood until the publication of Keynes's *General Theory*. Unlike the *Economic Consequences of the Peace*, the *General Theory* was concerned with an economy that was decidedly not in its Eldorado phase. Indeed, capitalism was rapidly approaching the very debacle Keynes had all along feared. His main preoccupation now was with developing a theory to explain the mass unemployment of the 1930s and to suggest the proper economic policies for restoring the economy to full employment. He was immersed in the *short run*, where the stock of capital could be taken as given. In this context the distribution of income was pushed into the background. It was not until the last chapter of the *General Theory* that Keynes returned briefly to the distribution of income and reversed himself completely from the position he had taken earlier in *The Economic Consequences of the Peace*.

Chapter 24 was titled "Concluding Notes on the Social Philosophy Towards which the General Theory Might Lead." The outstanding fault of capitalism was not only its "failure to provide for full employment," it was also "its arbitrary and inequitable distribution of wealth and incomes."[3] Indeed, the two were linked, although Keynes did not fully spell out the connection, nor did he provide as Michal Kalecki was later to do a full blown theory of the distribution of income based on a theory of oligopoly pricing (where Postulate I would no longer apply).[4] Keynes now reconsidered the necessity of an unequal distribution of income for an adequate rate of capital accumulation.

First, he claimed that progressive income and death duty taxes had gone far since the end of the nineteenth century to remove the "very great disparities of wealth and income" of an earlier age. But he was not willing to go along with the belief that a continued reliance on such taxes would diminish the growth of capital by weakening the capitalist's motive for individual saving. He went further. He now denied that "a large proportion of [the growth of capital was] dependent on the savings of the rich out of their superfluity." In the classical world, Say's law guaranteed the long-run equilibrium of the economic system at full employment, and any short-run deviation from that blissful state of affairs would be quickly corrected by automatic forces. Under such circumstances, capital accumulation would correspond with a relatively lower level of consumption, and an increase in the rate of capital accumulation would require a further lowering of consumption than would otherwise be the case. In Keynes's *General Theory*, however, a full-employment economy would be a matter of happenstance. Keynes now argued that with the economy at less than full employment, a low overall propensity to consume would hold back the growth of capital.

The next step in the argument was to relate the propensity to consume to the distribution of income. It is not the case, said Keynes, that high death duties "are responsible for a reduction in the capital wealth of the country." Insofar as the proceeds of high death duties would allow the government to lower its direct taxes on incomes, a move toward greater equality in the distribution of income would "increase the habitual propensity to consume" and thus "serve to increase at the same time the inducement to invest." Or, more generally, fiscal policy could be used to affect the distribution of income as part of its aim to increase the levels of real output and employment. It does not follow, under conditions of less than full employment, that a more equitable distribution of the social product in favor of labor (i.e., a decrease in the proportion going to profits) necessarily slows down the rate of capital accumulation in a self-defeating way. Indeed, the opposite is more likely to be true given capitalism's natural tendency toward deflation.

Although Keynes acknowledged that significant inequalities of income and wealth could be psychologically justified, the "large disparities as exist to-day" could not. Keynes's position on this matter was unequivocal:

> Thus our argument leads towards the conclusion that in contemporary conditions the growth of wealth, so far from being dependent on the abstinence of the rich, as is commonly supposed, is more likely to be impeded by it. One of the chief social justifications of great inequality of wealth is, therefore, removed.[5]

This represented a complete turnabout for Keynes, compared to his earlier analysis in *The Economic Consequences of the Peace*. The distribution of income may be a short-run parameter of the consumption function, but it can easily be turned into a positive policy variable. Since workers generally spend all of what they get, any forced redistribution of income to the laboring classes would serve to increase the overall propensity to consume and hence increase real output and employment by increasing aggregate demand, leading to a possible increase in the level of profits as well. Whether the magnitude of this redistributive effect would be large enough to achieve full employment is open to serious doubt. What is not is that it would in some measure, however limited, contribute to the solution and that an increase in the maldistribution of wealth and income would serve only to aggravate an already bad situation, perhaps seriously.

Perversely and in a nostalgic yearning for a return to earlier pre-Keynesian times, supply-side "theorists" in the first four years of the Reagan administration sought to promote capital accumulation and growth by cutting down on consumption via a redistribution of income away from labor to capital. It was a return, once again, to the pre–World War I habit of linking the rate of growth to the profits of a presumably low-consumption, high-saving capitalist class. It was not difficult to find these new "theorists" scolding degenerate capitalists for living too high on the consumption hog.[6] Growth, it was argued, is contingent on a fiscal policy that will cut down on consumption by swinging the distribution of income sharply in favor of the traditional capitalist class while putting pressure on unions to comply.

In the meantime, mainstream, neoclassical Keynesians continue to putter either with general equilibrium models which avoid the entire problem by arguing that capitalism has a natural, long-run tendency toward full employment, or with fine-tuning models designed to achieve artificially what cannot be brought about naturally. The end result, in either case, is the same. The curse of unemployment as a long-run tendency either does not exist or it can easily be dealt with on a policy level. The circle has been completed. It is against the counter-revolutionary complacency of neoclassical Keynesian theory and the retrograde theories of supply-side economics that Post Keynesian economics takes its stand.

Post Keynesian surplus economics

The neo-Ricardian school of modern Post Keynesian economics bases itself on Piero Sraffa's 1960 monograph, *The Production of Commodities by Means of Commodities*.[7] Picking up on Sraffa's total rejection of neoclassical marginal productivity theory, the neo-Ricardians have developed an analytical core that can most accurately be described as "Surplus Economics."

Any economy, if it is to be viable, must at the minimum be able to reproduce itself, i.e., it must be able to meet the subsistence needs of its people and to provide for the replacement of the preexisting capital stock used up in the process of production. Anything above these two basic replacement requirements is *surplus*. The distribution of this surplus between capitalists (who own the physical means of production) and workers (who sell their labor time to the capitalists) is basically a power relationship strongly biased in favor of the capitalists. It is the resulting skewed distribution of wealth that determines the distribution of income which, in turn, provides the power to demand certain goods and services—thus determining the allocation of resources along with commodity prices and factor incomes. In short, contrary to neoclassical theory, producers' (not consumers') sovereignty reigns supreme. It is the maldistribution of wealth and the class structure of society that determines prices, not supply and demand in competitive markets. More specifically, prices are a markup, on the basis of oligopoly market power, over an historically set wage level, itself the result of a struggle between capital and organized labor over relative shares. The theory of distribution, therefore, takes priority over an historically timeless neoclassical theory of subjective value operating in the vacuity of general equilibrium analysis.

Post Keynesians strongly object to the notion of a production function on the ground that, unlike the value of land and labor, the value of the capital stock cannot be determined independently of the distribution of income. As a result, the entire marginal productivity edifice of neoclassical theory collapses. This was the celebrated capital controversy of the 1960s.

Physical capital (the actual means of production) was not a homogeneous lump of putty; it was differentiated and beyond aggregation in value terms. The various "present-value" methods of capital valuation would not do because they required that the rate of interest be known beforehand, whereas it was the purpose of the theory to *determine* the rate of interest, not assume it—the rate of interest being the rate of profit or, in other words, the wages of capital. In short, the rate of profit could not be determined independently of the distribution of income. Neoclassical theory, in effect, assumed what it sought to prove.

The Italian branch of the Cambridge Surplus School, in particular, bases itself on Ricardo's distinction between the extensive and intensive margins and the Ricardian theory of differential rent that follows from this distinction. It is the level of employment that simultaneously determines the amount and quality of land brought into production, with the rent of the marginal land set at zero. This is the extensive margin, as distinct from the intensive margin where diminishing returns for homogeneous land set in with each increase in the intensity of cultivation—the neoclassical case. In Ricardo, land is not homogeneous; it involves different qualities of coexisting land. In that case "the Ricardian theory of extensive rent does not require any consideration of 'marginal changes.' "[8] Indeed, neoclassical marginal productivity theory does not apply at all.

The argument can be just as easily applied to capital. If one interprets the marginal efficiency of capital schedule extensively, the "ranking of all investment projects in a decreasing order of profitability is more akin to Ricardo's ranking of all lands in a decreasing order of fertility than to any marginal economic elaboration. And . . . there is absolutely no need to consider Keynes's marginal-efficiency-of-capital schedule as an expression of the marginal productivity of capital."[9] The neoclassical inverse monotonic relationship between the capital–labor ratio and the rate of interest (profit) is no longer necessary. In effect the *expected* yields of capital are taken to be independent of the market rate of interest. The important point is that investment demand is to be treated as a variation on the Ricardian theme of extensive rent rather than as a representation of neoclassical marginal productivity theory.

The net result is to call into question the very notion of factor demand curves.

To apply Ricardian rent theory to capital is to emphasize that capital is *heterogeneous* and to reintroduce the Marshallian notion of quasi-rent. It is the *entirety* of capital in all its heterogeneity, and not a part of it or a mass of undifferentiated capital as in neoclassical theory, that is important. In any event, the idea of a neoclassical aggregate production function using homogeneous capital is banished forever, as is the meaningless notion of the marginal productivity of capital and the competitive theory of distribution based on it.

Power in a class-structured society with a skewed distribution of wealth is what drives the capitalist system. It is the distribution of wealth and income that must serve as the starting point in the evaluation of any modern capitalist society. The distribution of wealth and income cannot be derived, as neoclassicists are wont to do, from the setting of prices in competitive goods and factor markets without doing gross violence to the world as it is. Prices, to repeat, are a function of the distribution of wealth, not the other way around. And the distribution of wealth mirrors the social and economic power structure of society.

As important as the Surplus School of Post Keynesian economics is, it is more Ricardo–Sraffa than it is Keynes, who, throughout his career, was a monetary economist involved with the major short-term problems of his times. In the Surplus School there is no credit-money economy. There is only the *real* world with its "central tendencies" and its immutable "centers of gravity." Its preoccupation is with the long run and with determining the internal logic of the capitalist system and whither it is going. It is the noumenal world that counts, not the ephemeral, phenomenological world of our everyday existence. The preoccupation of Surplus economists with a theory of objective value, "normal" prices, and centers of gravity has disturbing metaphysical overtones. As are their neoclassical counterparts, they are wedded to some notion of "equilibrium" as their basic tool of analysis and are struggling to discover the gravitational "laws" of capitalism. In doing so they largely ignore the historical transformations of capitalism and the changing political and sociological structures associated with these, at times, turbulent transformations.

Post Keynesian monetary economics

Keynes, himself, had no truck with centers of gravity, central tendencies, or "normal" prices reflecting an objective theory of value. His was a world of flux and change. Above all, capitalism was seen to operate in a credit-money economy permeated with uncertainty. At bottom, the differences between Surplus and monetary Post Keynesians are differences of social philosophy. One is more radical in its critique, the other liberal and more concerned with making the system work better by reforming it. The two are reminiscent of the older and even more passionate arguments of a past generation between the "maximalists" and the "minimalists" and the controversy that swirled over the "revisionism" of Engels's former secretary, Eduard Bernstein. It is the old problem of "Revolution or Reform?"

Much has been written in the field of surplus economics. Post Keynesian monetary economics, on the other hand, is at looser ends and there is less agreement over its proper content. It is this branch of Post Keynesian economics that will make up the core of this book. American Post Keynesians, generally, see capitalism as constantly evolving in its structure, institutions, and social relations. All notions of "equilibrium" and "central tendency" are rejected out of hand. It is the innovations and adaptations of capitalism that command attention. Historical conditions and historical time take precedence over mechanical equilibrium models operating in logical time. And since capitalism is essentially and profoundly a credit-money economy, financial structures and their innovations over historical time are of prime importance (although there is some disagreement among Post Keynesian monetary economists over detail and emphasis). Money, in other words, is what binds the present and the future in a world of uncertainty. And it is with the concept of "uncertainty" that the next chapter begins this particular study of Post Keynesian monetary economics.

The overall concern of the remaining chapters will be with the controversial issue of the demand for money as viewed by neoclassical Keynesians, monetarists, and Post Keynesians, along with the even more controversial concept of the supply of money. Keynesians and monetarists both regard the money supply as exogenous and subject to control by the central bank. What they disagree about is how that control should be exercised and by means of what instrumentality—free reserves or nonborrowed reserves? Post Keynesians, on the other hand, view the money supply as endogenous in that it will, one way or another and to a greater or lesser extent, accommodate the needs of trade no matter what, within limits, the central bank does.

In its most extreme formulation, it is a reverse twist on Say's law. Some Post Keynesians come close to arguing that in the monetary sphere *demand creates its own supply* automatically and in full through the accommodations of the central bank acting as lender of last resort. If, as is more likely, the central bank only *partially* accommodates increases in the demand for money, then movement will take place *along* the velocity curve through the activation of idle balances and the economizing of transaction balances. As the interest rate rises, however, *shifts* in the velocity function will also take place through the medium of financial innovations.

The controversial concept of money-supply endogeneity will be taken up in Chapters 4 and 5 where the concept of velocity will loom large in the reformulation of Post Keynesian monetary theory (of the less extreme variety). A final chapter will trace the development of monetary policy in the postwar period in terms of the doctrines, theories, and controversies covered in the earlier chapters. Throughout all this, money will be seen to be "peculiar"—as the next chapter will explain—and the overall conclusion will be that any theoretical analysis of a modern capitalist economy that does not take into account this peculiarity of money and the financial institutions through which it operates over time must, of necessity, be arid and with little relevance to things as they are. Overall, it will be argued, the policy implications of Post Keynesian monetary theory lead, inexorably, to the conclusion that selective control over the flow of credit in the economy must augment an effective and permanent "incomes policy" if capitalism is to remain viable in the long pull. Yet questions remain as to the political feasibility of the American Post Keynesian policy prescriptions and their avoidance of the fundamental problem of the distribution of the surplus product within a capitalist system, particularly at a time when government policy seeks to change it radically in favor of capital. At any rate, conventional monetary and fiscal policies alone cannot do the job, as has been amply demonstrated over most of the postwar period.

In what follows, the basic tenets of American Post Keynesian economics must be kept clearly in mind. They are: (1) the pervasiveness of uncertainty as distinct from calculable risk; (2) the historical time within which production and all other economic events take place in an irreversible fashion; (3) the existence of a credit-money economy of forward contracts in which the money supply has virtually a zero cost of production; (4) the setting of individual product prices as a mark-up over unit prime costs in the dominant oligopolistic sector operating with *planned* excess capacity; (5) the irrelevance of demand–supply analysis to labor markets, and the key dependence of the general price level on nominal wage rates determined exogenously under collective bargaining; (6) the endogenous nature of the money supply;

and (7) the inherent instability of capitalism.

All these propositions are deeply interrelated and feed on one another. They form the basis of a devastating critique on neoclassical economics. All of them will be covered in one form or another in the chapters that follow.

Notes

1. See Jean de Largentaye, "A Note on the *General Theory of Employment, Interest and Money*," *Journal of Post Keynesian Economics*, Spring 1979.

2. John Maynard Keynes, *The Economic Consequences of the Peace* (New York: Harcourt, Brace and Howe, 1920), pp. 10–11; subsequent quotations are from p. 12 and pp. 18–22, italics supplied.

3. John Maynard Keynes, *The General Theory of Employment, Interest, and Money* (New York: Harcourt, Brace, 1936), p. 372.

4. See Michal Kalecki, *Selected Essays on the Dynamics of the Capitalist Economy* (New York: Cambridge University Press, 1971), Ch. 6.

5. Keynes, *General Theory*, p. 373.

6. See, for example, George Gilder, *Wealth and Poverty* (New York: Basic Books, 1981). For a critical evaluation of supply-side economics, see Stephen Rousseas, *The Political Economy of Reaganomics: A Critique* (Armonk, N. Y.: M. E. Sharpe, Inc., 1982).

7. Cambridge University Press. Sraffa, who died in 1983, was well known as the editor of the collected works of David Ricardo and for his celebrated "Introduction" in Volume 1 of the series (London: Cambridge University Press, 1951) as well as for his earlier, 1926 article on "The Laws of Return Under Competitive Conditions" (*Economic Journal*), which opened the way for Joan Robinson's theory of imperfect competition. A good introductory volume to surplus economics is: Peter M. Lichtenstein, *An Introduction to Post-Keynesian and Marxian Theories of Value and Price* (Armonk, N. Y.: M. E. Sharpe, Inc., 1983).

8. Alessandro Roncaglia, *Sraffa and the Theory of Prices* (Chichester: John Wiley & Sons, 1978), p. 106.

9. Luigi Pasinetti, *Growth and Income Distribution: Essays in Economic Theory* (London: Cambridge University Press, 1974), p. 43.

CHAPTER 2

The peculiarity of money

Uncertainty in historical time

One of the basic assumptions of Post Keynesian monetary theory is that we live in a world of uncertainty. A second assumption, implied by the first, is that all events take place in historical time. Historical time, furthermore, is seen as being irreversible. We do not have the luxury of doing something and, not liking the way it turns out, ask that we be allowed to start all over again, wiping out all the vestiges and consequences of our first try. Decisions to act, once implemented, tend to unfold along lines we do not expect. Commitments, in other words, are not easily undone and they are invariably undertaken in a penumbra of indeterminateness. They have a way of starting a chain of events that have an element of surprise in them. We are, consequently, forever trapped in the present, in a historically contingent world in which the future is largely unknown and unforeseeable. The only thing we can say with any assurance is that the future unfolding of events cannot be predicted, that what we *expect* to happen will most likely not happen. Being so, we must always be in the process of adapting our strategies to changing circumstances, again without any guarantee that our new-laid plans will work out any better than before; and so on *ad infinitum* as a new train of events unfolds conditioned by our newly developed responses to the unpredictable events occurring in an ever-shifting present.

How we try to cope with uncertainty defines the system under which we live. Capitalism has one way of doing it, socialism another. And it is the capitalist response to uncertainty that gives money its peculiarity. Orthodox economics assumes the problem away. It assumes either that a given state of always realized expectations exists over time, or that uncertainty can be converted to "certainty" by recourse to the calculus of probability. Uncertainty either does not exist, in this schema, or it can easily be reduced to calculable "risk." Rational decision making can then go its merry "scientific" way, as in that scene in Evelyn Waugh's *Brideshead Revisited* where "the doctor spoke dispassionately, almost brutally, with the relish men of science sometimes have for limiting themselves to inessentials, for pruning back their work to the point of sterility."

Neoclassical economists base their theories on ideational "facts" with all the trappings of science. Having established the "science" of economics in all its inessentials, their next step is to indoctrinate the next generation in their ways. As the anarchist-philosopher Paul Fayerabend[1] has put it: "Scientific education . . . simplifies 'science' by simplifying its participants." The domain of research is not only defined; it is "separated from the rest of history . . . and given a logic of its own." The historical process is frozen in an all-pervasive world of certainty, and time now becomes *logical* time operating within a framework of equilibrium analysis that allows it to flow backwards as well as forward. With the "standards of argumentation" set, the well-trained epigones engage themselves in the endless task of paradigm polishing. It is a task that assumes a static universe with a well-defined underlying structure in a state of rest. The noumenal and the phenomenal worlds merge. This state of rest, or stable equilibrium, is the end product of *tatônnement*. Bids and offers are made for an existing supply of goods and, when prices that clear all markets are finally arrived at, the process stops and exchange takes place. All factor and goods prices having been firmly established, they become the basis for recontracting that guarantees the clearing of all markets. All participants in the system now know their costs and their revenues with certainty. Uncertainty disappears from view and business hums along in a blissful state of general equilibrium ruled by "impersonal Reason" in the form of "rational Man." The "facts" of the system are seen as natural, not historical, phenomena; and they assume a timeless universality.[2] Neoclassical theory, in other words, deals with capitalist uncertainty by defining it out of existence.

Keynes on uncertainty

Although Keynes, in his *Treatise on Money* (1930), based much of his analysis on "bulls" and "bears," there is little on "expectations" or "uncertainty," as such. Indeed, in the index of his two-volume work there is no entry for either concept and the "Bulls-Bears" and "Two Views" entries deal largely with speculation on the stock exchanges. The *Treatise* was a half-way house between Keynes's *Tract on Monetary Reform* (1923) and his *General Theory of Employment, Interest, and Money* (1936).

His analysis of expectations in relation to output and employment, in the *General Theory*, focused on the long-term expectations that govern the pace of investment. The *expected* rate of profit of any investment project was seen to depend on the current supply price of a capital asset and its prospective yield. The problem, however, was not with the supply price, which firms could estimate with reasonable accuracy. Keynes was more concerned with "the extreme precariousness" of any estimate of prospective yield. It is "a characteristic of human nature," he wrote, for decisions "to depend on spontaneous optimism rather than mathematical expectation." And this "spontaneous urge to action rather than inaction" is ultimately "a result of animal spirits— . . . not as the outcome of a weighted average of quantitative benefits multiplied by quantitative probabilities." In the final analysis, "whim or sentiment or chance" governs our actions in a world of uncertainty.

Keynes's most trenchant statement on uncertainty, however, is to be found in his response, a year later, to the largely negative reviews of the *General Theory*.[3] Replying to his critics, Keynes focused on what he thought distinguished the *General Theory* from orthodox economics and elaborated further on what have been called the "dark forces of time and ignorance." Widening the distance further between himself and classical economists, he criticized their assumption that expectations could "be given a definite and calculable form." This conversion of uncertainty into "risk" reduced "uncertainty to the same calculable status as that of certainty itself." Keynes disassociated himself from this approach. For him, uncertainty took on a darker coloration.

> By "uncertain" knowledge, let me explain, I do not mean merely to distinguish what is known for certain from what is only probable. The game of roulette is not subject, in this sense, to uncertainty . . . The sense in which I am using the term is that in which the prospect of a European war is uncertain, or the price of copper and the rate of interest twenty years hence, or the obsolescence of a new invention . . . *About these matters there is no scientific basis on which to form any calculable probability whatever. We simply do not know.* (Pp. 213–214, italics supplied)

Orthodox economists, according to Keynes, overlooked "this awkward fact" by assuming that simple extrapolations from the past were reliable guides to the future—*natura non facit saltum*, as Alfred Marshall wrote on the flyleaf of his *Principles*. Behaving on the basis of this belief that nature does not move in great leaps only serves to strengthen the "forces of disillusion" leading to "sudden and violent changes." "I accuse the classical economic theory," he wrote, "of being itself one of these pretty, polite techniques which tries to deal with the present by abstracting from the fact that *we know very little about the future*" (p. 215, italics supplied). Indeed, the orthodox theory of the future was a "false rationalization" leading to "a wrong interpretation of the principles of behavior" and to "an underestimation of the concealed factors of utter doubt, precariousness, hope and fear" (p. 222).

Uncertainty and time

Apodictic certainty clearly has no role to play in any accurate accounting of human experience. In a sense, all history is Terror—of the unknown. The future is unknowable; it involves a dialectic that is open-ended and *a priori* indeterminate. And it exists in historical time.

All decisions, being temporal, take place over time and are made on the basis of an *expected* future. The "celestial mechanics" of neoclassical equilibrium theory, wherein all individual actions are prereconciled into a rational coherence,[4] becomes irrelevant. Movement exclusively along stable and independent functions is inadmissible, as is the notion of a stable equilibrium that follows from such narrowly conceived movements. Abrupt shifts and the interdependence of schedules are the rule not the exception. Comparative statics becomes the plaything of a bankrupt system straining to cope with uncertainty without actually bringing it openly into the analysis. In a world of uncertainty and historical time, decisions are *ex ante*; outcomes are *ex post*. And it is in this realm of time and uncertainty that decisions are made concerning output and investment and, in consequence, the level of employment. Entrepreneurs operating in the present must make decisions concerning what and how much to produce, the types and amount of capital to be combined with labor in the production of a particular good (which will depend on the cost of capital relative to the wages of labor), and the unit or sale price at which the final product will be sold.[5] All these decisions are made with no assurance, in a world of uncertainty, that they will be the right ones. Along the way, continual periodic adjustments will have to be made as the future becomes present and the present past. Households will face similar problems basing current consumption and savings on an expected income stream that is itself uncertain and based, in large part, on the decisions made in the production sector.

Neoclassical theory, on the other hand, deals essentially with a barter economy operating under conditions of certainty. Money is brought in as an afterthought, if at all—either in the form of manna from Heaven or, as Milton Friedman would have it, from a helicopter. Or, it can be in the form of one commodity serving as *numéraire*, or a commodity money (gold and silver) where there is a production function for money whose response to an increase in demand "will depend on the nature of its elasticity of supply *in terms of goods*."[6] There is no provision for a monetary system interacting with the real sector of the economy. When money is brought in, it is often in the form of the quantity theory of money where the money supply is *exogenously* determined by the central bank. And changes in the money supply are seen, in the long run, to affect only the level of prices with no lasting effect on real output and employment—which is at rest in a state of full-employment equilibrium.

In a credit economy, by contrast, money has no supply function in the production sense. The volume of money existing at any one time largely depends on the net level of bank lending. It is not neutral, particularly in an economy operating under conditions of uncertainty. Entrepreneurs and households, moreover, enter their commitments on the basis of contracts denominated in money. The monetary system therefore plays a critical role in the operation of the economy, and understanding the functioning of a credit-money economy is therefore critical for any analysis of contemporary capitalism.

A major point emphasized in Post Keynesian monetary theory is the role played by forward contracting as a means for coping with an uncertain world. Given the inherent volatility of expectations, capitalism has developed a way of containing the *ex post* surprises associated with *ex ante* decisions in the production sphere. Capitalism's response to uncertainty is planning in the private sector while deploring it in the public sector. It is a private form of "incomes policy" for an economy in which production takes place over time.

There are various ways of coming to terms with uncertainty in a capitalist system. A key way is through monopolistic concentrations of market power through vertical and horizontal integration, conglomerate mergers, product differentiation, and still other ways of amassing economic power. Almost any industrial organization textbook would provide an abundance of examples, but the use of *private* capitalist planning to cope with uncertainty has been lucidly described by John Kenneth Galbraith in his popular *New Industrial State*. The more prominent Post Keynesian monetary theorists, unfortunately, have downplayed this aspect of dealing with uncertainty and have, instead, concentrated on the notion of a "forward contract." To them, it "is the most important economic institution yet devised for controlling the uncertain future course of markets."[7] These contracts are used to determine future sales prices as well as the input prices of labor and working capital (materials costs). They are a form of wage and price controls that convert uncertainty into relative certainty, not by a probabilistic analysis but by reaching into time, via forward contracts, to guarantee future prices and costs. One of the more critical forward contracts is that covering labor costs. Without long-term wage settlements, arrived at through collective bargaining, entrepreneurs would be hard put to undertake the long-run commitments necessary for production to take place.

If capitalism, because of uncertainty and the irreversibility of time, is inherently unstable, then forward contracting explains its apparent stability over time by artifically achieving a relative stability of expectations. Without forward contracts, the argument goes, life under capitalism would be violently unstable. But contracts imply the existence of courts to enforce them. The role of the state therefore becomes critical in seeing to it that the "rules of the game" are followed. Should there, for any reason, be a disruption of the existing legal and governmental framework, then "a catastrophic breach in the continuity of the system is inevitable" and a modern monetary economy is faced with violent instability and possible political collapse.

"The swing of a physical pendulum," wrote A. C. Pigou, "progressively contracts under the influence of friction, but we cannot infer from this that the swing of a psychological pendulum will do so."[8] The first half of the sentence more properly refers to the celestial equilibrium mechanics of neoclassical theory; the second half to an economy operating under the Post Keynesian conditions of uncertainty and unstable expectations. Once the psychological pendulum starts swinging there is nothing inherent in the system that will necessarily bring it back to a state of tranquil rest. Unless the arc of the swing can somehow be contained, the system could well be ripped apart. In that sense, forward contracting is a critical element of Post Keynesian analysis, particularly in an economic system that is in a state of *permanent disequilibrium* as it moves inexorably through uncertain time.

In summary, the essential nature of a capitalist society is not harmonious, automatically tending, within a system of supposedly competitive markets, toward a long-run equilibrium at full employment. On the contrary, it is based on subjective expectations in a world of uncertainty and is therefore inherently unstable since "mistakes" are bound to be made. Capitalism, consequently, is unavoidably cyclical in nature and the concept of a long-run equilibrium—at hand or in the distant future—is illusory and misleading. The basic difference between those who adhere to the neoclassical synthesis of "bastard" Keynesians (or the monetarism of Milton Friedman) and those who belong to the Post Keynesian camp is that the latter have gone back to the pre-bowdlerized, original ideas of Keynes in order to achieve a neo–Post Keynesian synthesis based on uncertainty.

The peculiarity of money

It should be emphasized that in a fundamental sense uncertainty in a capitalist system is to be found in its production relationships, which are governed by the private ownership of the means of production. Even though individual units try to cope with uncertainty via *private* planning, the composite production of the whole of society is nevertheless unorganized and uncoordinated, with each individual striving to grab as large a market share as possible. It is this "anarchy of capitalist production," to use a Marxian phrase, that gives rise to uncertainty, and the persistence of uncertainty under capitalism follows from the unwillingness of capitalists to tolerate an effective system of compensatory or direct governmental planning. Despite the concentration of market power and forward contracting as a means of coping with it, uncertainty is always present in a fundamental and inescapable way. It is in this sense that the concept of uncertainty provides a deep insight into the inherent instability of a capitalist system.

As important as forward contracts may be in the production sector, they serve only to confine uncertainty within tolerable limits; they do not do away with it entirely. Financial forward contracts also leave a large residual uncertainty in place. Their existence, however, is negligible by comparison, especially for short-term money market instruments, which, by the very nature of their shortness, are liable to marked variations in interest income as short-run interest rates change in response to market forces; or, to put it more succinctly, they are subject to income uncertainty while maintaining a large degree of price certainty. In a nonbarter monetary economy, it is the continued presence of uncertainty in all markets, to a lesser or greater extent, that permits money to serve as a *store of wealth* or *value*, that is, to be used as a hedge against uncertainty. In the total absence of uncertainty, as Keynes emphasized, there would be no need to hold cash balances in excess of transaction needs. All idle balances would be automatically converted into long-term earning assets and the use of money as a store of wealth would not exist. It is primarily the uncertainty about the future course of interest rates that leads to the use of money as a store of value. Were it not for the existence of uncertainty, "Why," asked Keynes, "should anyone outside a lunatic asylum wish to use money as a store of wealth?"[9]

It is, in other words, the very existence of uncertainty in a capitalist system that gives money its "peculiar" quality. As G. L. S. Shackle has argued, it allows decisions to be *deferred* in the sense of "avoiding commitments to technically specialized, hazardous types of assets."[10] Money, he continues, is "the postponer of the need to take far reaching decisions" by virtue of the liquidity that money provides. It is, to put it otherwise, *the temporary abode of purchasing power in a world of uncertainty*. In the words of Keynes, "A monetary economy . . . is essentially one in which changing views about the future are capable of influencing the quantity of employment and not merely its direction," and in such an economy, "money enters into the economic scheme [of things] in an essential and *peculiar* manner."[11]

Another peculiarity of money is that it has no production function, in the conventional sense of that term. And if we take into account the wide spectrum of highly liquid financial assets (near monies), with their high elasticities of substitution and low transactions costs, we have at hand a powerful force which, as we shall see in subsequent chapters, makes a mockery of monetary policy and the notion that the money supply is exogenously determined by the central bank.

There remains the distinction to be made between financial assets and real assets, a distinction that clearly separates Post Keynesian monetary theorists from quantity-theory monetarists. Short-term financial assets are held both for the income they yield (especially at high interest rates) and as a highly liquid store of wealth that can be quickly converted into money proper (cash plus checkable deposits) in established spot markets at nominal cost. Real assets, on the other hand, are not liquid and cannot serve as a store of wealth. They can rarely be sold quickly, nor is their sale value as assured as it is for short-term financial assets; nor is there a high elasticity of substitution among such real assets as specialized capital equipment, land, furniture, housing, and the like. To the extent that resale markets for real assets exist, they are thin. It is the peculiarity of money and near monies (which are being rapidly converted into interest-paying checkable deposits) that makes the income velocity of circulation of the money supply such a critical factor in the working of a modern monetary economy. And with the violent transformation of the monetary system via financial innovations, it is the state of *general liquidity*, rather than the narrower concept of the money supply, that has become the critical factor in the oscillations of the economy. The money supply, however defined, has now become *endogenous* and, as we shall see in Chapters 4 and 5, this notion of an endogenous money supply becomes one of the critical building blocks of Post Keynesian monetary theory, although considerable confusion surrounds it in the Post Keynesian literature.

Money is, indeed, peculiar, but what is even more peculiar is the failure of conventional theory to recognize the full dimension of its importance in the operation of a capitalist economy; and in those few cases where an attempt has been made to bring money explicitly into orthodox theory, the results have been invariably disastrous.[12] They have little, if any, relation to the real world of capitalism.

Money and debt

In a larger context, there is yet another peculiarity of money in that it makes monetary debt possible. Financial contracts, as distinct from forward contracts covering the prices of goods and inputs, relate debtors to creditors. According to Hyman Minsky, who has almost single-handedly pioneered this field,[13] firms, households, and government undertake a variety of financial postures, which he grouped into three categories: hedge, speculative, and Ponzi financing. Briefly put, lenders give up potential purchasing power in the form of money in exchange for a stream of future income that may or may not be realized; uncertainty prevails. The honoring of the debts thus created depends on the ability of borrowers to meet their financial commitments over time, that is, on a stream of cash flows sufficient to validate the financial commitments of borrowers. Each type of borrower has a main source of cash "which is expected to accrue so that the financial instruments it has outstanding [i.e., that the borrower has issued to lenders] can be validated" (p. 21). For households it is wages and for government, taxes. For nonfinancial firms, *expected* gross profits generate the needed cash flow, and for financial corporations "it is the cash flow from owned contracts."

Hedge financing exists when the expected gross profits exceed the payment commitment, that is, when a margin of safety exists. Significantly, hedge financing "is not directly susceptible to adverse effects from changes in financial markets" (p. 26). Bankruptcy becomes a possibility only when the margin of safety disappears, that is, when *realized* gross profits are less than the contracted interest income to be paid out to the lender. *Speculative financing* implies that although the expected gross profit may be less than the payment commitments *for some periods of time*, refinancing will be available to meet the shortfall of those deficit periods—with the expected cash flows of later periods able not only to repay the original short-term loan but the subsequent refinancing loans as well. Or, in Minsky's terms, "a speculative unit finances a long position in assets by short run liabilities" (p. 27). The danger in speculative financing, to which hedge financing is not subject, is that an increase in short-term interest rates will apply to refinance loans and may thus keep the sum total of payment commitments chronically above the projected future cash flows of the investment project, at least temporarily until interest rates decline again at an appropriate time. Finally, *Ponzi financing* is speculative financing caught in the bind of chronically rising short-term interest rates over the full course of the investment project. The borrower is now forced periodically to take out additional short-term payment commitments (loans), at successively higher interest rates, to meet the rising interest payments in excess of gross profits, and the "outstanding debt grows even if no new income yielding assets are acquired" (p. 28). Ponzi financing is trapped in a double bind of increasing costs—those due to the rise in short-term interest rates and those due to the forced increase in the size of the debt over time. The dilemma of the foreign debts of Brazil, Mexico, and Argentina in 1983 is a case in point.

Minsky uses his three-tiered schema of financing to generate an endogenous theory of the business cycle. The divisions between the three types of financing are not clear cut or immutable, and the stability of a monetary economy based on debt depends on the mixture of the three types, and the shift of financing along this spectrum. For example, a shift of central bank monetary policy from targeting interest rates (Federal Funds) to targeting the monetary base (nonborrowed reserves) to fight inflation would result in a large increase across the spectrum of interest rates pushing hedge financing into speculative and speculative into Ponzi financing. Or, alternatively, if some exogenous shock to the system (the OPEC crisis) should induce a severe recession, expected gross profits would fall dramatically leading to the same result, even if interest rates remained unchanged. In either case, the overall debt structure of the economy could not be validated because payment commitments in their aggregate would far exceed aggregate expected cash flows, and a general debt deflation would follow leading to a rash of business bankruptcies and bank failures.

In effect, this is a brief summary of Minsky's "financial instability hypothesis," in which "money is not just a generalized ration point that makes the double coincidence of wants [in a neoclassical barter economy] unnecessary for trading to take place; money is a special kind of bond that emerges as positions in capital assets are financed" (p. 61)—under conditions of uncertainty, one might add, which themselves guarantee the latent instability of a capitalist system. Money is "peculiar," therefore, because of its ability, in contrast to its function in standard economic theory, to destabilize the real economy. For Minsky, however, the central bank serving as a lender of last resort and the central government buttressing gross profits by deficit contracyclical spending have in concert prevented "It" from happening again. There are elements in Minsky's financial theory of the business cycle that are contrived, but his theory, controversial as it may be, does focus attention on the role of money and debt in a world of uncertainty.

The artificial restoration of Say's law

Although Minsky's financial instability hypothesis is grounded on the assumptions of Post Keynesian analysis, an earlier neoclassical approach to preventing "It" from happening again dominated most of the postwar years up to the 1960s. The trauma of the 1930s could not be allowed to happen again and with neoclassical Keynesian theory now firmly in place there was no need to repeat the experience. Fiscal and monetary policy were up to the task of keeping the economy on an even keel with the sea swells in output and employment now to be kept within politically tolerable limits. The business cycle could be tamed once and for all.

The case for an optimal mix of a conservative fiscal policy restricted to tax cuts and a nonliquidity trap version of monetary policy found its ultimate expression in the "fine-tuning" Keynesians who descended on Washington in the early and heady Camelot days of the Kennedy administration. This triumph of "bastard" Keynesianism was based on the wonders of the IS-LM analysis of Hicks, and Samuelson's promulgation of the neoclassical synthesis. As early as 1946, in a review of the *General Theory* on the occasion of Keynes's death, a brash and very young Samuelson[14] reflected on how remarkable it was that "so active a brain [as Keynes's] would have failed to make any contribution to economic theory" and how sad it was for Keynes "to have left no mark on pure theory"—"pure" theory, of course, meaning highly rarefied mathematical models. Moreover, "Keynes himself did not truly understand his own analysis" (a charge also made in a different sense by the more radical Joan Robinson). Although acknowledging the *General Theory*, a bit inconsistently, as "a work of genius," Samuelson went on to describe it as "a badly written book, poorly organized, . . . arrogant, bad-tempered [and] polemical"—properties generally absent, on the surface, from mathematical general equilibrium models, which, themselves an act of rude violence on "reality," reduced the *General Theory* to a mechanical contraption devoid of Keynes's insights on the workings of a capitalist society.

Samuelson grouped Keynes with Smith, Cournot, and Walras (with no mention of Ricardo, who, apparently in Samuelson's opinion, was not in the same class). Twenty-seven years later, as an appendage to his 1946 essay,[15] he placed himself and two others at the head of a *reconstructed* Keynesianism firmly embedded in the neoclassical synthesis:

> [I]n the writings of Solow, Tobin, and myself, attention was focused on a *managed* economy which *through the skillful use of fiscal and monetary policy* channeled the Keynesian forces of effective demand *into behaving like a neoclassical model.*

The idea of artificially prodding the economy "into behaving like a neoclassical model" through the "skillful use of fiscal and monetary policy" in a "managed" economy is no less than dragging Say's law into the analysis through the back door. Joan Robinson and Frank Wilkinson were pitiless in their critique:

> The old orthodoxy, against which the Keynesian revolution was raised, was based on Say's law—there cannot be a deficiency of demand . . . Keynes pointed out the obvious fact that investment was governed by the decisions of business corporations and public institutions, not by the desire of thrifty households to save . . . According to the bastard Keynesian doctrine, it is possible to calculate the rate of saving that households collectively desire to achieve; then governments, by fiscal and monetary policy, can organize this amount of saving. *Thus Say's law is artificially restored and the old doctrines creep back again* . . . The bastard Keynesians [have] turned the argument back into being a defense of *laissez-faire,*

provided that just the one blemish of excessive saving was going to be removed [that is, by Samuelson's "skillful use of fiscal and monetary policy"].[16]

Keynesian demand management foundered in the decade of the 1970s. Up to that point it had been based on a consensus politics respected by both Democratic and Republican administrations, where differences that did exist between them were differences in emphasis. Throughout the postwar period the improved distribution of income over the pre-war and pre-Depression periods was not allowed to deteriorate through the government's concentration of social expenditures over a broad range of transfer payments. In that way government expenditures served as a corrective for the more unequal distribution of income that would have followed from the underlying inequality in the distribution of wealth.

Liberal Keynesianism avoided Keynes's original support of the socialization of investment in favor of the fine-tuning to be achieved by Samuelson's "skillful use of fiscal and monetary policy." It represented a form of welfare capitalism that skirted the conflict between capital and labor inherent in a capitalist system. Its success, however, required a sustained rate of economic growth at a relatively full-employment level of output if the problem of the distribution of income were to be depoliticized. It was the collapse of the Western economies in the aftermath of the 1973–74 OPEC crisis (compounded by the Iranian revolution of 1979) and the onset of "stagflation" that posed a problem neoclassical Keynesians could not handle. Their underlying support crumbled and the way was cleared for a new approach in the 1980s that, using a generally discredited incentive theory, proposed a supply-side type of fiscal policy designed to redistribute the social product back to capital at the expense of labor—while at the same time adopting a counterproductive monetarist approach to monetary policy. The consensus politics of the postwar period was shattered and "Keynesianism without tears," as A. C. Pigou called it, had had its day.

Notes

1. Paul Fayerabend, *Against Method* (New Jersey: Humanities Press, 1975), pp. 17–28.

2. *Cf.* Maurice Merleau-Ponti, *Humanism and Terror* (Boston: Beacon Press, 1969); original French edition published in 1947.

3. "The General Theory of Employment," *Quarterly Journal of Economics*, February 1937.

4. See G. L. S. Shackle, *The Years of High Theory* (London: Cambridge University Press, 1967).

5. For a fuller discussion of this point, see Paul Davidson, *Money and the Real World*, 2nd ed. (New York: Macmillan, 1978).

6. Nicholas Kaldor, *Origins of the New Monetarism*, The Page Lecture delivered at University College, Cardiff, December 30, 1980 (Cardiff: University College Cardiff Press, 1980), p. 15, original italics.

7. Davidson, *Money and the Real World*, and Paul Davidson and J. A. Kregel, "Keynes's Paradigm: A Theoretical Framework for Monetary Analysis," in Edward J. Nell, ed., *Growth, Profits and Property*, Ch. 8 (New York: Cambridge University Press, 1980).

8. *Keynes' General Theory: A Retrospect* (London: Macmillan, 1950), p. 63.

9. "The General Theory of Employment," p. 216.

10. Shackle, *Years of High Theory*.

11. *General Theory*, Preface, p. viii, italics supplied.

12. For a useful survey of the various attempts to introduce money into modern growth theory, see Jac. J. Sijben, *Money and Economic Growth* (Leiden: Marinus Nijhoff, 1977), and my review in *Kyklos*, Fasc. 1, 1978.

13. See his collected essays in *Can "It" Happen Again?* (Armonk, N. Y.: M. E. Sharpe, Inc., 1982).

14. Paul Samuelson, "The General Theory," *Econometrica*, July 1946; reprinted in Robert Lekachman, ed., *Keynes' General Theory: Reports of Three Decades* (New York: St. Martin's Press, 1964).

15. Lekachman, *Keynes' General Theory*, italics supplied.

16. Joan Robinson and F. Wilkinson, "Employment Policy," *Cambridge Journal of Economics*, March 1977, italics supplied.

CHAPTER 3

The demand for money and the rate of interest

The exogenous money supply

Within traditional Keynesian economics money serves as a means of payment and a store of wealth. These two functions of money were used by Keynes to undermine the classical dichotomy between the real and monetary sectors of the economy. The end result was his liquidity preference theory of the demand for money which allowed changes in the monetary sector to be transmitted to the real sector through changes in the rate of interest. But Keynes also assumed, along with everyone else, that the *supply* of money was exogenously determined. An exogenous money supply is simply another way of saying that the central bank (through its use of open market operations, the discount rate, and reserve requirements) can adjust the overall volume of money, in response to changes in the demand for it, to that level consistent with its policy objectives.

In a tight money situation, neoclassical Keynesian analysis, as we shall see, did allow that certain short-run leakages could occur, via changes in the income velocity of money in response to interest-rate changes, that would tend to undermine the effectiveness of a monetary policy operating directly on the supply side. Such leakages, however, were believed to play themselves out quickly, allowing the full effectiveness of monetary policy to take hold in sufficient time to achieve the policy objectives of the monetary authorities. Monetarists, on the other hand, deny that the central bank can effectively use *discretionary* monetary policy in the short run. The variable lags of monetary policy, in conjunction with the inability of anyone to locate the actual position of the economy on the business cycle, at any particular moment of time, make it impossible, according to the monetarists, for the central bank to control the exogenous money supply in a contracyclical manner. Indeed, central bank policies are notoriously perverse in achieving *ex post* what was not intended. For monetarists the only sensible thing to do is to ignore the short-run business cycle altogether and play for the long run. The greatest contribution the central bank can make, in their view, is to allow the money supply (which is presumed to have a stable relationship to the monetary base, i.e., the sum of bank reserves and currency in circulation) to increase mechanically at the natural, long-term growth rate of the economy adjusted for the secular decline in the income velocity of money—the famous "monetary rule." But whether one opts for the monetarist rule or the Keynesian use of short-run discretionary monetary policy with the rate of interest as its target, the fact remains that *both* regard the money supply as exogenous; it is not determined endogenously within their respective systems. With the money supply thus determined "outside" the system, the demand for money becomes the center of attention.

From a Post Keynesian perspective the idea of an exogenous money supply is contrafactual. It is an heroic assumption at best that will be left unexamined until Chapter 4, although it will be touched upon briefly in the analysis of Keynes's finance motive in this chapter.

The demand for money within the industrial and financial sectors

Keynes's liquidity preference theory was very much within the Cambridge "money sitting" tradition which sought to explain *why* "people" in the aggregate choose to hold a certain proportion (k) of nominal income (Y) in the form of money. It was a portfolio approach to the demand for money as a stock.

In terms of the earlier and more familiar Cambridge equation, $M = kY$ where k is the money-income ratio or the reciprocal of the income velocity of money (V). Income, in this schema, becomes a function of the money supply, which is another way of saying that the causal arrow runs *from M to Y*. Moreover, if in the long run the economy naturally tends toward a unique equilibrium at full employment, then the price level is also uniquely dependent on the money supply in an equiproportionate manner. And a change in the exogenous money supply, in this model, would have no effect on the real sector of the economy or on the rate of interest—the latter being determined exclusively by the relation of productivity and thrift in the real sector. The rate of interest was seen as the "reward for abstinence," which at increasing interest rates generated the funds (savings) to be applied to investment by reducing, to an equivalent extent, the amount allocated to consumption. The interest rate determined the *composition*, not the level, of aggregate real output. It functioned in the same manner as Maxwell's demon in the second law of thermodynamics: it equilibrated and kept constant the temperature of the economy at the automatically attained ideal level of full employment.

It was, of course, this fiction that Keynes exploded in his *General Theory*, and he did so by denying the validity of the quantity theory of money. A key element in his attack was his insistence that the interest rate was a monetary phenomenon which spilled over into the real sector through the marginal efficiency of capital schedule. Although he minimized the role of monetary policy in the *General Theory* in favor of fiscal policy, it was subsequently reconstituted in the bowdlerized, neoclassical version of his theory—or what Joan Robinson referred to as "bastard" Keynesianism. At any rate, for Keynes, the interest rate was a reward for parting with *liquidity*, not for abstaining from consumption.

The motives for holding money were the transactions (and precautionary) motive for holding active balances to be used as a means of payment (L_1), and the speculative motive which led to the demand for idle balances as a store of wealth (L_2). As a first approximation, L_1 was seen to depend exclusively on the level of economic activity (Y), and the demand for money as a store of wealth (idle balances) was in turn dependent on the state of expectations concerning the future course of the rate of interest (i), which, in a world of uncertainty, could not be known *a priori*.

Keynes's formulation of liquidity preference in the *General Theory*, however, was a watered down version of his richer analysis of the demand for money in the *Treatise*. It should be emphasized that Keynes, throughout his career, was a monetary economist. All his major works had to do with money, from his *Indian Currency and Finance* (1913) to his *Tract on Monetary Reform* (1923) to his two-volume *Treatise on Money* (1930) to his shattering *General Theory of Employment, Interest, and Money* (1936). Keynes was steeped in the real world and his knowledge of the City and the workings of the Treasury were profound. He had little patience with economists who spun out rarefied, abstract theories that reveled in the internal, logical consistency of their systems—while doing violence to the real world.

Had he never written the *General Theory* his reputation in the history of economic thought would have been assured by the *Treatise* alone. Although the *Treatise* was fundamentally neoclassical in its theoretical core, its observations on the working of the economy were rich in illustrations taken from the real world. His knowledge of the financial world was profound, and his treatment of the demand for money flowed directly from it.

In the *Treatise* Keynes began by distinguishing between *Industry* and *Finance*. His definitions were clear cut.[1]

> By *Industry* we mean the business of maintaining the normal process of current output, distribution and exchange and paying the factors of production their incomes for the various duties they perform from the first beginning of production to the final satisfaction of the consumer.

> By *Finance* . . . we mean the business of holding and exchanging titles to wealth . . ., including Stock Exchange and Money Market transactions, speculation and the process of conveying current savings and profits into the hands of entrepreneurs.

Keynes's next step was to explain the use of bank deposits in two distinct spheres—or what he called *Industrial Circulation* and *Financial Circulation*. In the sphere of industrial circulation, the *income deposits* of households arise out of the imperfect synchronization of receipts and expenditures, i.e., the interval between the two and the difficulty of at least some individuals to foresee the "precise date of either." These income deposits are periodically replenished out of personal income and are used to meet personal expenditures and savings. In addition to income deposits, individuals also hold a certain amount of cash for their transactions needs.

Analogously, *business deposits* used in the sphere of production are also the result of an imperfect synchronization of receipts and expenditures which leads to the holding of "temporary balances of cash or bank-deposits." They represent the "proceeds of sales to consumers" and are used to pay for the factors of production employed in the industrial sector. Moreover, income deposits flow constantly into this type of business deposit in payment for the purchase of goods "and out again through payment of wages" into the income deposits of consumers. The rate of turnover of income deposits, however, is considerably smaller than for production business deposits, or what Keynes called *Business-deposits A*. The ratio between the two velocities, or their turnover rates, is exceedingly variable—the reason being that while income deposits experience a "regularity in the dates of payment," business-deposits A have no such regularity; that is, in a world of *uncertainty* expected sales can veer widely from actual sales.

The sum of income and business deposits in the industrial sector made up what Keynes called *cash deposits*, which are used exclusively to meet transactions requirements for a means of payment in that sector. The volume of cash deposits over time can vary because of changes in (1) "the character of production," (2) "the habits of the public and the business world," and (3) "the sacrifice involved in keeping resources in the form of money." And as Keynes emphasized elsewhere in the *Treatise* (Vol. 1, Ch. 13), changes in the distribution of income between wages and profits could serve as a fourth category. Yet "the aggregate of money incomes, i.e., . . . the volume and cost of production of current output," is far more important in determining variations in the demand for cash deposits.

Financial sector payments, on the other hand, are met by two types of deposits—*business-deposits B* and *savings deposits*. The volume of business-deposits B depends on "the volume of trading in financial instruments, i.e., the *activity* of financial business." Financial business deposits, however, are highly variable and *are not closely related or dependent upon the level of economic activity in the industrial sector*. Their turnover rate, moreover, is very large although their absolute variation is small because of clearing arrangements in the financial sector, e.g., on the stock exchange.

Savings deposits, as with business deposits, are broken down into two components: *savings-deposits A* and *savings-deposits B*. Savings-deposits A, or passbook savings, are held for personal reasons and are extremely stable as a result. It is savings-deposits B which fluctuate with the changing balance between "bears" and "bulls." In contemporary terms, they can be equated with highly liquid negotiable certificates of deposit (CDs), money market funds, and the like. "Bears" anticipate a fall in the cash value of financial securities and increase their holding of savings-deposits B, whereas "bulls" represent movement in the opposite direction from money to securities. The demand for money in the financial sector is the sum of business-deposits B and savings-deposits B—"with the fluctuations in Savings-deposits B . . . probably the most important element in the variability of the financial money demand."

The important point is that although cash deposits in Industrial Circulation are directly related to the pace of the economy in the production and consumption sectors, the demand for financial deposits depends "on the comparative attractions *in the mind of the depositor* of [savings-deposits B] and of alternative securities" (italics supplied). Consequently, the ratio between cash deposits and financial deposits is liable to erratic and therefore unpredictable fluctuations. Uncertainty plays a far greater role in the financial sector of the economy and explains its higher and largely unrelated volatility. Since the total demand for money is the combined demand of the industrial and financial sectors, and since the two depend on different motives for holding money—the demand for money as a means of payment and the demand for money as a store of wealth—*Keynes denied any stable link between money and the nominal level of national income.* In direct contradiction to the monetarist position of fifty years later, he emphatically rejected what has become one of the main tenets of the "revised" quantity theory of money.

Restricting himself to "cash deposits" Keynes argued that the velocity of income deposits was relatively stable while that of business-deposits A was not. He attributed the larger variation of business-deposits A velocity to the greater irregularity of payments in the business world, the tendency of businessmen to economize on their transactions balances in times of rising interest rates, and the greater variation in business habits and practices. In terms of the *General Theory* the greater volatility of business expectations in a world of uncertainty was the prime reason for the different velocities of income deposits and business deposits in the industrial sector. Keynes's position in the *Treatise* was unequivocal (p. 49, original italics):

> [I]t is misleading to represent the *total* cash deposits (i.e., income-deposits *plus* business deposits) as bearing any stable or normal relationship to the national money-income.

And in a broader and more contemporary context, given the even greater volatility of financial deposits—as they spill in and out of the industrial sector—the variability of the overall income velocity of money would further preclude any stable link between the volume of money and money-income.

Keynes, in the *Treatise*, was also concerned with the conflicts that could exist between the industrial and financial demands for money and the dilemma such conflicts would pose for the monetary authorities. A speculative boom in the financial sector, given the total money supply, could well end up "stealing resources from the industrial sector." If the central bank refused to accommodate the financial sector, interest rates would rise causing "an immediately deflationary tendency" in the industrial sector leading ultimately to a fall in real output and a rise in unemployment. If, on the other hand, the central bank increased the money supply to meet an excessive financial demand for money, interest rates would remain low but the speculative "bull" market would continue unabated, as it did in 1929, leading finally to a crash of the economy as a whole. With a runaway speculative bubble, the demand for business-deposits B would soar and there would be little the central bank could do in light of their offsetting "very high velocity of circulation." To react to the problem with a high interest rate policy could lead to a major deflation, as would the passive accommodation of the financial sector's demand for additional money.

Keynes, considerably ahead of his time, was willing to meet the problem head on by discriminating "in terms of lending (either the rate charged or by rationing the amount) between the financial and industrial borrowers"—in other words, by recourse to *selective* controls over the flow of credit between the industrial and financial sectors (which the Federal Reserve System pointedly refused to do in the 1920s "bull" market) as an alternative to either a high interest rate policy or accommodative increases in the money supply. These are important issues to be elaborated upon in Chapter 6.

The finance motive

One year after the publication of the *General Theory*, Keynes extended his theory of the demand for money in what have now become three celebrated articles.[2] He made even clearer the importance of uncertainty in the real world in a way that undercut his own use of equilibrium analysis in the *General Theory* and was reminiscent of the prevalent disequilibrium approach of his *Treatise*.

In his June 1937 *Economic Journal* article, and in another article six months later in the same journal, Keynes introduced the notion of a finance motive which was to be a part of the total demand for money in addition to the L_1 and L_2 demand functions. The concept of time was made explicit. Firms make at least some of their investment decisions *ex ante*, which generate a "temporary demand for money before it [actual investment] is carried out." This particular demand for money is "quite distinct from the demand for active balances which will rise as a result of the investment activity whilst it is going on." It involves a *planned* investment for which "financial provision" will have to be secured "*before* the investment takes place," that is, an "advance provision of cash . . . required by the current decisions to invest." For Keynes this was an addition to the traditional transactions demand for money and was seen to be of special importance during an investment boom. It would appear, therefore, that the finance motive demand for transactions balances applies to the immediate or very short run period and is transient in nature. The heavy demand for investment finance in such a case could possibly "exhaust the market" since at the *ex ante* planning stage no net saving will have "taken place, just as there has been no net investment." This "temporary" demand for money to "finance" the projects would be particularly large in the sphere of industrial circulation. The lack of "financial facilities" on reasonable terms would become problematical and serve in the very short run as a brake on "the pace of new investment."

The critical question is what happens to the supply of money in the face of such an increase in the demand for *ex ante* finance? If the central bank were "unwilling to increase the supply of money and the supply from existing holders is inelastic," investment decisions could not be validated because of the exhaustion of available finance. The first half of the quotation refers to the policy decision of the monetary authorities not to accommodate the increased *ex ante* demand for transactions balances attributable to the *ex ante*, planned increase in autonomous investment. The second half, however, assuming the supply from existing holders to be *perfectly* inelastic, implies that the income velocity of money is at its maximum value—that is, idle balances have been exhausted and the economizing of transactions balances has been taken to its outermost limit. A further implication is that in the absence of financial innovations, which in any event cannot occur in the immediate short run, the underlying financial structure is stable. There can therefore be no accommodation of the increased demand for money through increases in the velocity of money as an offset to the central bank's refusal to increase the stock of money. Under these circumstances it is indeed "the financial facilities which regulate the pace of new investment." It would seem to follow from Keynes's argument that *external* sources for the financing of planned investment (the financial sector's provision of loans—debt—or absorption of equity) have been "exhausted" and are simply not available. In other words, the planned investment relevant to the finance motive is over and above that part that has been already financed from the internal funds of firms (accumulated depreciation reserves and undistributed profits) *and thus actualized*. It can therefore be assumed, in this instance, that the investment boom has exhausted internal funds as well and that a residual of planned investment remains to be financed, constituting the unrequited finance demand for money.

In his December 1937 article, however, Keynes offered another explanation that has been taken up by Post Keynesians in arguing for the full endogeneity of the money supply. Although Keynes was more concerned in this article over his dispute with Bertil Ohlin on the relation of savings to investment—whether saving determines investment or whether, as Keynes argued, investment determines the level of savings—he returned once again to the finance motive and its possible effect on the rate of interest. Keynes posited the existence of an *interregnum* "between the date when the entrepreneur arranges his finance and the date when he actually makes his investment." During this interregnum "there is an additional demand for liquidity without, as yet, any additional supply of it arising."

Finance, to Keynes, is a "revolving fund." With investment proceeding at a steady rate, "the flow of new finance required by current *ex ante* investment is provided by the finance released by current *ex post* investment." But when *ex ante* investment greatly exceeds the flow of *ex post* investment, the problem of finance asserts itself full force. During the *short-run* interregnum period " 'finance' is wholly supplied . . . by the banks," and it is this fact that makes "their policy . . . so important in determining the pace at which new investment can proceed," and since the central bank determines the amount of finance that banks have to offer, it is central bank policy that plays the key role in determining the *pace* of investment.

To summarize: a burst of *ex ante* investment results in a marked increase in the demand for *ex ante* finance "which cannot be met without a rise in the rate of interest unless the banks are ready to lend more cash . . . at the existing rate of interest," which is unlikely. The role of the banking system is therefore critical in the "*transition* from a lower to a higher scale of activity" (italics supplied). If there is inadequate accommodation of the demand for *ex ante* finance, congestion will take place on "the short-term loan market" and the pace of investment will be severely constrained.

It was at this point that Keynes raised the issue of unused overdraft facilities, which has become so popular with some Post Keynesians.

[*T*]*o the extent that the overdraft system is employed and unused overdrafts ignored by the banking system*, there is no superimposed pressure resulting from planned activity over and above the pressure resulting

> from actual activity. In this event the transition from a lower to a higher scale of activity may be accomplished with less pressure on the demand for liquidity and the rate of interest. (Italics supplied)

If the overdraft facilities were without limit, the interest rate would remain unchanged and the supply of money would be perfectly elastic.

In his earlier June article, Keynes stressed the importance of the finance motive when he wrote, "I should (I now think) have done well to emphasise it when I analysed the various sources of the demand for money." The fact is, however, that the finance motive comes into play primarily during a charged expansion of the economy leading to abnormal increases in planned investment. Under normal circumstances and over a long period of time, the finance motive would not be a significant component of the total demand for money, and to the extent that it did exist it would be a "temporary" demand due in time to disappear as the needed savings materialized, or as a result of increases in the income velocity of money due primarily to financial innovations induced by the tight monetary policies of the central bank—or as the outcome of a fully accommodative central bank, which is counter to the notion of an exogenously determined money supply.

A formal model of the finance motive

The model to be presented will show the special assumptions and limitations that underlie the finance demand for money in the immediate short run, particularly in view of the heavy emphasis it has been given in some corners of Post Keynesian theory, particularly by Paul Davidson.[3] We begin with a simple two-sector Keynesian model based on the following elementary equations for consumption and investment:

$$C = a + cY \qquad (1)$$

and

$$I_r = b - di \qquad (2)$$

where c is the marginal propensity to consume, I_r is the actual, or realized, investment that has been successfully financed and has therefore taken place, and i is the market rate of interest governing the actual level of investment.

Combining equations (1) and (2) yields the equilibrium level of national income (Y_e), namely:

$$Y_e = k(a + b - di) \tag{3}$$

where the multiplier $k = 1/(1 - c)$.

At any given moment of time, the equation for the total demand for transactions balances (L_T) is given by:

$$L_T = \lambda_1 C + \lambda_2 I_r \tag{4}$$

where λ_1 represents the demand for transactions balances by the consumption sector and λ_2 the transactions demand of the investment sector. Moreover, λ_1 and λ_2 are dependent on the pattern and frequency of payments in each sector, and the underlying financial structure within which both sectors operate is taken to be stable in the very short run. Given the different habits and customs of consumers and businessmen, it can be safely assumed that λ_1 and λ_2, although roughly stable within the limits of 0 and 1, are not equal.

The model also assumes that in the immediate short run the interest rate (i) is given along with the marginal propensity to consume (c) and that all the remaining parameters of the consumption and investment functions are similarly frozen. Substituting equations (1) and (2) into equation (4), we get:

$$L_T = [\lambda_1 a + \lambda_2(b - di)] + \lambda_1 cY = (\lambda_1 a + \lambda_2 I_r) + \lambda_1 cY \tag{5}$$

where $\lambda_1 a + \lambda_2 I_r$ represents the intercept of the linear L_T function and $\lambda_1 c$ its slope.

The model next introduces the traditional Keynesian demand for transactions balances (L_t), which is taken to be a stable function of the level of economic activity (Y); i.e.,

$$L_t = mY \tag{6}$$

where m is the reciprocal of the transactions velocity of money, and the existence of equation (6), as distinct from equation (5), follows from the assumption that λ_1 and λ_2 are not equal. Equation (6), moreover, is a straight line through the origin, the slope of which represents a constant transactions velocity of money $(\overline{V}_1)$.

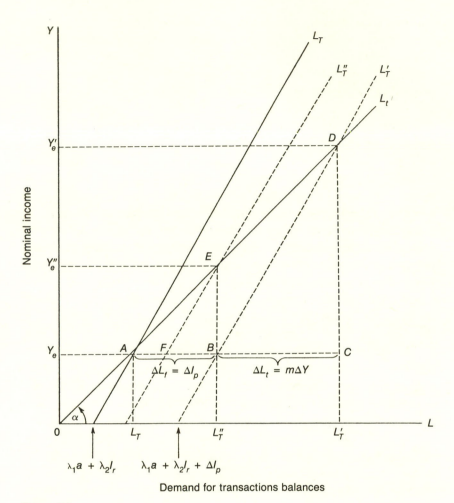

Figure 3.1

Figure 3.1 plots equations (5) and (6). The L_t curve represents a locus of equilibrium points, i.e., potential points at which the system is at rest after the dust of getting there has settled. Which particular point on the L_t curve will prevail at any one time depends on the location of the L_T curve—which in turn depends on the values assumed for the various parameters in equation (5). Given these parameters, which also yield the corresponding equilibrum level of output (Y_e) by equation (3), the intersection point of the two curves is preordained. In Figure 3.1 the L_t and L_T curves intersect at point A. At this initial equilibrium point there is no finance motive demand for transactions balances since all planned investment of the previous time period will have been realized with, as will be shown, the full cooperation of the central bank. The demand for transactions balances is therefore exactly equal to its supply.

The stability of the system at point A, however, is not automatically maintained by the countervailing pressure of purely economic market forces. The stability of the equilibrium point A requires that whenever a deviation takes place the central bank will in all instances act with dispatch to restore the economy to its original equilibrium level of output at Y_e; that is, an excess demand or supply of money will not be tolerated. A further valiant assumption is that the central bank has the power and the requisite tools to achieve its policy objectives. The economy's remaining at point A is therefore uniquely dependent, all other things given, primarily on an all-powerful central bank behaving effectively in a prescribed manner. But this prescribed manner, as will be shown, is contrafactual; it is impossible to attain. Point A is therefore, in fact, anything but stable.

The effect of an increase in autonomous investment

As is clear from equation (5), the L_T function includes within it the parameters of the consumption and investment functions. Therefore, any change in any of the parameters of C or I will cause a *shift* in the L_T function. To illustrate the finance demand for money, we will assume a change in b, one of the two parameters of the investment function.

An increase in b to b' will therefore result in a rightward autonomous (i.e., parallel) shift of the investment function, taken to represent, in the immediate short run, the increase in *ex ante* or planned investment (ΔIp). Whether or not ΔIp can be realized in fact, however, depends on the availability of finance. For the moment, at any rate, no increase in the level of output has actually taken place; i.e., in actual terms $\Delta Y = 0$ and Y remains at Y_e in Figure 3.1.

In keeping with Keynes's original formulation of the finance motive, it is assumed that the central bank, initially, is holding the money supply fixed at that level consistent with Y_e in Figure 3.1 and that "the supply from existing holders is [perfectly] inelastic." The resulting "exhaustion" of available finance comes at a time when the internal funds of firms have already been used up by the intensity of the investment boom. In such a case $\lambda_2 = 1$, which is another way of saying that the economy is at a point where the unrealized increase in *ex ante* or planned investment (ΔIp) has, via Keynes's finance motive, resulted in an exactly equivalent increase in the finance demand for transactions balances (ΔL_f). The increase in the b parameter of the investment function therefore implies, since b is also a parameter of the L_T function, a parallel shift to the right of the total demand for transactions balances exclusively in terms of Keynes's finance motive.

Figure 3.1 shows the parallel shift of the L_T function from L_T to L_T'. The L_T function now becomes:

$$L_T' = [\lambda_1 a + \lambda_2(b - di) + \Delta b] + \lambda_1 cY$$
$$= (\lambda_1 a + \lambda_2 I_r + \Delta I p) + \lambda_1 cY \tag{7}$$

Subtracting equation (5) from equation (7), we get:

$$\Delta L_T = \Delta I_p = \Delta L_f \tag{8}$$

i.e., the increase in the demand for transactions balances is, initially, exactly equal to the increase in the finance demand for money. This is shown in Figure 3.1 by the segment AB. But that is not the end of the story. The supply of money must be brought explicitly into the analysis.

The first question to be asked is: What will happen on *the supply-of-money side*? Will the increased demand for *ex ante* finance (ΔL_f) be satisfied and by whom and under what conditions? What if it is not? What are the consequences in either case? We assume, in what follows, that overdraft facilities are negligible or nonexisting. The focus therefore is on the central bank. If the central bank holds the economy at point A by refusing to accommodate ΔL_f, then that is the end of the matter since there cannot be any indirect accommodation via ΔV in the model. We are stuck at point A and the L_T' curve becomes irrelevant. If, however, a more reasonable and politically sensitive central bank should initially increases the supply of money by the amount $AB = \Delta L_f$, certain further consequences will follow. As the increased financial demand for money is accommodated, planned investment will become actualized. Assuming it is done in one fell swoop, ΔI_p will be instantaneously transformed into ΔI_r and the multiplier will swing into action. From equation (3) we get:

$$\Delta Y = k\Delta b = k\Delta I_r \tag{9}$$

and from equation (6) we get:

$$\Delta L_t = m\Delta Y \tag{10}$$

i.e., the satisfaction of ΔL_f by the central bank will generate an induced increase in the demand for transactions balances as the economy moves in Figure 3.1 from point A to point D—where the corresponding equilibrium level of output is Y_e'. The *total* increase in the demand for transactions balances (ΔL_T^*) now becomes the sum of the financial demand for money and the induced increase in demand due to the central bank's accommodation of ΔL_f, or:

$$\Delta L_T^* = \Delta L_f + \Delta L_t = \Delta I_r + m\Delta Y \qquad (11)$$

In Figure 3.1 ΔL_T^* is shown as the segment AC which is the sum of AB and BC, with AB representing $\Delta L_f = \Delta I_r$ and BC representing $\Delta L_t = m\Delta Y$. In short, the new equilibrium position at point D cannot be reached unless the central bank fully and automatically accommodates not only the finance demand for transactions balances (AB), but the induced demand for money (BC) as well. The important point is that at D the economy is once again in a "stable" equilibrium position where the "temporary" financial demand for money (having been met and then some by the central bank) now disappears from view, and the total demand for money is once again equal to its supply—there being, as at point A, no remaining excess demand to be satisfied by a compliant central bank now holding the money supply fixed at that level consistent with Y_e'.

But what if the central bank limited itself to restricting its increase in the money supply to the extent only of the initial increase in the demand for money, i.e., by the amount ΔL_f? What, in other words, will happen if there is only a *partial* accommodation of the total increase in the demand for transactions balances $(\Delta L_T^* = AC)$ by the amount AB? In that case the drive to get to point D will generate an unrequited excess demand for money equal to BC. In consequence, the interest rate will now rise and, assuming velocity to be at its maximum value, there will be no indirect increase in the money supply; i.e., the increase in the money supply is restricted to the partial accommodation by the central bank, AB. At the higher interest rate, investment will fall as the economy moves up its given investment demand curve, as will the demand for finance money as a result. The consequent fall in the demand for finance money is shown in Figure 3.1 by the shift to the left of the L_T' curve to L_T''.

As shown in Figure 3.1, the finance demand for money falls by the amount BF leaving the net increase in the demand for finance money at AF. As AF is actually used for the reduced level of real investment, the

economy via the multiplier effect moves to point E and its corresponding income level of Y_e''. The total increase of the money supply by the
central bank (AB) is now absorbed by the reduced finance demand for
money (AF) plus the corresponding induced demand for transactions
balances (FB) as the more limited increase in investment becomes
actualized. The system is in equilibrium at point E, with the increased
supply of money (AB) equal to the total increase in the demand for it. In
short, *partial* accommodation by the central bank will abort the movement of the economy from A to D and bring it to rest at the intermediate
point E.

In his 1937 articles, Keynes made it clear that he regarded the
demand for finance money as a "temporary" phenomenon that came
into play during an investment boom. Failure to meet that demand by an
uncooperative central bank *operating within an inelastic credit structure* could affect the pace of investment and hence the level of real
output and employment. But Keynes did not assume a perfectly elastic
money supply, for if the money supply is automatically endogenous all
along the line, then the finance motive becomes a trivially ephemeral
and unimportant novelty. It takes on importance only in the case of non-
or partial accommodation because of their potential impact on the level
of real output and employment (points A and E in Figure 3.1 rather than
point D). Under less extreme circumstances, moreover, where the
financial structure retains some of its elasticity, the finance demand for
transactions balances could be met, even with an uncooperative central
bank, by induced changes in the rate of interest and consequently in the
income velocity of money. Even under boom conditions, however, the
internal cash flow of corporations (undistributed profits plus depreciation accruals) is generally greater during a developing upsurge and
could, if the need were pressing, be further increased by oligopolistic
corporations through an increase in their markup over unit prime costs,
thereby generating an increase in internal funds and diminishing the
importance of the finance demand for money from the banking system.
There is a danger that the emphasis put by some Post Keynesian
"monetarists" on the finance motive has been greatly exaggerated; that
it is much ado about very little.

It could be argued, alternatively, that Keynes did not fully seize the
opportunity that his concept of the finance motive provided. His theory
of liquidity preference in the *General Theory* was a step back from his
analysis of the demand for money in the *Treatise*. It was essentially a
bond-money model where the demand for money was a demand for
earning assets. The finance motive, however, focused on the demand

for money not as a demand for a stock of assets but as a business demand for a *flow of credit*. It concerned the *industrial* sector and its pursuit of profit through investment and the process of capital accumulation. It is not so much the *demand* for money that takes primacy, but the flow of credit-money to the industrial sector that is of critical importance in analyzing a capitalist system.

Yet care should be taken not to exaggerate the role of banks in the investment process. The ability of the banking system to affect the pace of investment is a short-run phenomenon that comes into play only in exceptional circumstances. Under normal conditions, the *ex ante* demand for money would be largely financed out of some combination of corporate internal funds and excess bank liquidity. As planned investment became actualized, the increased demand for transactions balances (due to the multiplier effect of investment on the level of economic activity) would be met out of the increased savings associated with the higher levels of income—with any shortfall being made up either by the central bank or, at higher interest rate levels, by induced changes in the income velocity of money via the activation of idle balances and by financial innovations. To put the greater onus on banks for any unrequited investment is to miss the point.[4] And to argue that the central bank fully accommodates any and all increases in the demand for money not only overstates the case but eliminates banks as a barrier to increased investment. If blame is to be apportioned properly, most of it should go to central banks captured by monetarist counterrevolutionaries. Money does matter in the short run and it does affect the level of investment, and hence output and employment, when, on a mistaken notion of the cause of inflation, its quantity is severely restricted.

The income velocity of money

In Keynes's original formulation of the demand for money, the income velocity of money could not be taken for granted. Keynes in the *General Theory* was not a quantity theorist. As early as his *Tract on Monetary Reform* he had serious doubts about the stability of velocity. And in his *Treatise on Money* these doubts became even more pronounced. Since the demand for financial deposits was more related to the highly psychological and unstable "bearish" and "bullish" sentiments of the public with regard to the future price level of securities, and not to the level of economic activity in the industrial sector, the link of the general price level to the quantity of money "is not of that direct character which the old-fashioned quantity equations . . . might lead one to suppose.'' Still, Keynes argued that in a full-employment equilibrium the quantity theory of money and its equiproportionality requirement would hold.

In the *Treatise* this was recognized only as "a theoretical possibility." In the real world of actual events "*the degree of change in the quantity of money, the velocities of circulation, and the volume of output will not be related in any definite and predictable ratio to the degrees of change in the fundamental price-levels.*" In the *General Theory*, as in the *Treatise*, the quantity theory applied in a full-employment equilibrium. But since this was only one of an infinite number of possible equilibrium points, the chances were overwhelming that it would not be applicable in real-life situations. The relation between money and prices was one of "extreme complexity" and, argued Keynes in the *General Theory*, it is not at all clear "as to which variables [in the quantity theory of money] are taken as independent." For the quantity theory of money to apply, we would have to assume a static society operating under conditions of certainty. With the total absence of uncertainty, the L_2 demand for idle balances would be zero—there being no uncertainty as to the course of future interest rates, it would be madness to hold idle balances in the form of cash. In that case the supply of idle balances would be zero and the total money supply would consist of transactions balances; i.e., when $M_2 = 0$, $\bar{M} = M_1$. There being no propensity to hoard, the economy must be at full employment; and with the level of output given and $M_2 = 0$, Keynes argued, "it follows, if we can take V also as constant, that . . . the price-level will be directly proportional to the quantity of money." But in the real world of uncertainty V cannot be taken as constant, and, within Keynes's liquidity preference theory, velocity is uniquely dependent on the rate of interest.

In the *General Theory*, the *Treatise*'s demand for money in the industrial sector (cash deposits) becomes the demand for transactions balances (L_1). It is dependent mostly on the level of economic activity in nominal terms (Y). In the *Treatise* the parameters for this demand function, as we have seen, were: (1) the character of production, (2) the habits of the public and the business world, and (3) the opportunity cost of holding cash balances, i.e., the interest income foregone. A fourth parameter should also be added to the three cited by Keynes, namely, (4) the underlying institutional structure of the financial sector of the economy and its stability, i.e., the absence of rapid financial innovations. Assuming all four to be constant, then the demand for transactions balances is determined by the current pace of production in the industrial sector, or $L_1 = L_1(Y)$.

In the *Treatise*, however, Keynes explicitly allowed the demand for "cash deposits" to respond to the rate of interest: "[W]hen business is active and the cost of borrowing high, firms will tend to *economize* in the amount of Business-deposits A which they keep" (italics supplied); that is, the velocity of circulation of Business-deposits A will rise. In the *General Theory*, Keynes toned this down to a "first approximation" in which L_1 is completely inelastic with regard to the rate of interest. The rate of interest was reserved for the dominant role it was to play in the L_2 demand function for idle balances held as a store of wealth—within which the financial sector of the *Treatise* was now to be found. The L_1 demand for money is shown in Figure 3.2 as a straight line through the origin with nominal income (Y) on the vertical axis and the demand for transactions, or active, balances (L_1) on the horizontal axis. The tangent of angle α is Y/L_1, which can be written as Y/M_1 since the transactions demand for money has priority over the L_2 demand for idle balances and is the first to be satisfied out of a given exogenous money supply—with the residual, M_2, remaining to satisfy the L_2 demand for speculative balances. The tangent of the angle is nothing less than the income velocity of transactions balances ($\bar{V}_1$), which is necessarily constant given the linear L_1 function going through the origin. In this schema, it is only the L_2 demand for money that is inversely related to the rate of interest. With the money supply exogenously determined by the central bank, and in the absence of any change in it ($\bar{M}$), any increase in the aggregate demand for money due to an increase in the level of economic activity could be satisfied only by an increase in the overall velocity of circulation. This can be shown in a simplified equation:

$$V = \frac{M_1\bar{V}_1 + M_2 V_2}{\bar{M}}$$

Since the velocity of M_2 is zero,

$$V = \bar{V}_1 \frac{M_1}{\bar{M}}$$

Therefore V can increase, given $\bar{V}_1$, only by an increase in M_1 via an equivalent decrease in the M_2 component of the given total money supply; i.e., since $\bar{M} = M_1 + M_2$ and $M_1 = \bar{M} - M_2$,

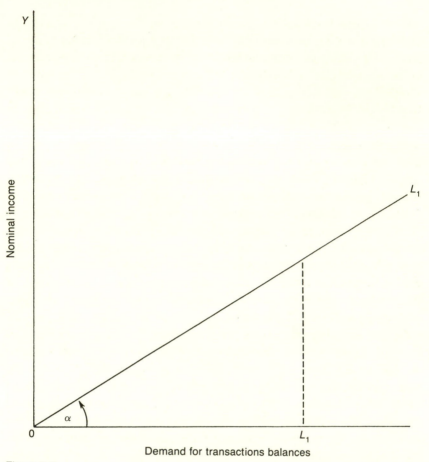

Figure 3.2

then $+ \Delta M_1 \equiv - \Delta M_2$, which implies an increase in the rate of interest as a result of the increase in the demand for M_1 (itself induced by an increase in the level of nominal income) in the face of a constant $\bar{M}$.

At some point, however, the supply of M_2 will be totally exhausted and $M_1 = \bar{M}$, with V now equal to $\bar{V}_1$. Any further increase in V requires an increase in V_1; i.e., the demand for transactions balances would have to become interest-sensitive. At the presumably high interest rate level that it would take to drive the demand for idle balances down to zero, businessmen (as Keynes observed in the *Treatise*) find the opportunity cost of their transactions balances so great that they "economize" by paring them down unto the bone. Overall velocity then increases by the amount of the increase in V_1, i.e., $\Delta V = \Delta V_1$ with $M_2 = 0$. The economizing of transactions balances, however, cannot go on forever. It is more limited in the role it can play in allowing V to increase than is the case for changes in M_2. Eventually it, too, must cease and overall velocity (V) will grind to a halt at its velocity maximum. This state of affairs to shown in Figure 3.3.

The $V(i)$ curve intersects the interest rate axis at the interest rate floor (i_f), which is some conventional rate above zero since in an uncertain world no money will be lent out, for obvious reasons, at a zero percentage rate. The curve slopes upward at an increasing rate as movement *along* the $V(i)$ curve takes place with each increase in the rate of interest. When all idle balances have been activated and the economizing of transactions balances has been exhausted, the $V(i)$ curve becomes infinitely inelastic at the maximum value of velocity (V_{max}). Corresponding to this V_{max} is some maximum value of nominal income (Y_{max}). If Y_{max} is seen to be excessive (inflationary), the central bank can increase the rate of interest by reducing the exogenous money supply. Monetary policy is thus seen, within a neoclassical Keynesian framework, as a potentially powerful contracyclical tool capable of setting Y_{max} equal to the desired, noninflationary level of national income (Y_e)—provided that the decrease in the money supply does not cause an offsetting *shift* in the $V(i)$ curve, i.e., provided that the underlying financial structure is not affected by the actions of the monetary authorities, a bold assumption at the very least.

Whether increases in the income velocity of money, for whatever reasons, are sufficient to fill the unaccommodated increase in the demand for money (i.e., the total or remaining excess demand for money) is a matter to be examined in later chapters. In the absence of financial innovations, however, velocity changes will eventually exhaust themselves and the velocity maximum will have been attained. When that occurs monetary policy becomes fully effective, or so the argument goes. If before the velocity maximum is reached, the monetary authorities find the changes in velocity troublesome, they can, the argument continues, always reduce the exogenous money supply to halt the inflationary process and achieve the level of nominal income they desire at a relatively stable price level. It is, in effect, the neoclassical Keynesian version of a stable demand curve for money—once velocity changes have worked themselves out or are counteracted by bringing the money wall into action if the velocity changes prove too big for comfort. What is being assumed, of course, is that the barn door can be shut before the horses run out. It is all very mechanical and that is where the fault lies. It is the Erector set version of Keynesian

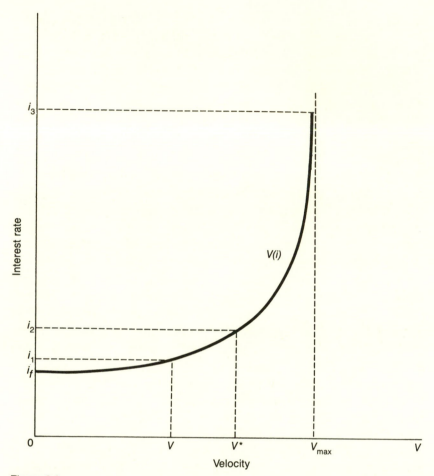

Figure 3.3

economics that became so popular in the postwar period up to 1973 when it collapsed in a state of confusion.

A markup theory of interest rate determination

Within traditional as well as neoclassical Keynesian theory, the rate of interest has served as an equilibrating force, or that particular variable that tied the whole system together in a neat, determinate package. In neoclassical Keynesian theory, the IS and LM curves of the Hicksian general equilibrium model were assumed to be independent of one another and, given their relative stability (which, in effect, pushed the problem of uncertainty aside), the level of real output and employment was determined. The model, of course, did admit the possibility of an underemployment equilibrium and was in that sense faithful to Keynes's major finding, but even that possibility was later denied by grafting to the model a classical real-wage labor market working in tandem with a real balance effect that guaranteed a unique long-run equilibrium at full employment.[5] No matter what form the model took, the intersection of the IS and LM curves uniquely determined the equilibrium rate of interest at which the money and goods sectors were in simultaneous equilibrium, with a simultaneous equilibrium in the labor market thrown in for good measure in the *pre*-Keynesian version of the *General Theory*. The rate of interest, in other words, was market-determined.

If, however, the psychological factors that underlie the IS and LM curves in a world of uncertainty make them, in fact, interdependent, the usefulness of the rate of interest as an equilibrating force quickly dissipates in a haze of indeterminateness. One way out of this conundrum, within a Post Keynesian framework, is to shift the emphasis from liquidity preference theory to credit-money and the role of banks. The best way of doing so is to apply Michal Kalecki's theory of markup pricing to the loan rates charged by banks for bank credit.[6]

Markup theory assumes an economy in which there are large concentrations of market power. As applied to the nonfinancial sector of production, oligopolistic firms operate at a *planned* level of excess capacity and the degree of monopoly in each industry allows a markup over unit prime costs. In the financial sector the interest rate is to be seen as the "price" of the financial "goods" provided by that sector. A markup theory of bank loan rates, as in the case for prices in the production sector, rejects the demand–supply analysis of competitive market behavior inherent in the IS-LM determination of the equilibrium rate of interest. An increase in demand relative to supply does not automatically transform itself into an increase in the loan rate. An "equilibrium" approach to the rate of interest charged by banks is not applicable to the financial sector.

It will be necessary, however, to translate the terms of markup pricing for real goods into their equivalents for the financial sector and to adjust the relative importance of the various components of markup theory. The markup equation for nonbank firms, $P = k(u)$, can be rewritten for commercial banks as $i = k(u)$, where i is the interest rate on loans, k the degree of monopoly or market power exercised by individual banks, or, in the aggregate, by the banking industry as a whole, and u the unit prime or variable costs incurred by banks.

The total costs of *nonbank* firms consist of certain fixed or overhead costs (including depreciation) and prime costs which vary with the level of output. Prime costs are the sum of the cost of labor (wage costs) and the cost of raw and intermediate goods (circulating capital) that enter into the production process. By their very nature, fixed costs per unit of output fall along a hyperbolic curve as output increases. Unit prime costs, often controlled by forward contracting, are relatively constant over the range of less than full capacity utilization that follows from the built-in planned excess capacity of oligopolistic firms. The degree of monopoly, or gross profit margin, which has been relatively stable over the long run, represents the markup over prime costs that determines the price of goods consistent with the profit goals of firms.

Demand and supply have little, if anything, to do with the setting of oligopolistic commodity prices. An increase in demand, unless viewed as a permanent phenomenon, will elicit an increase in output by cutting into the planned excess capacity of oligopolistic firms with no effect on prices in the short run. Price changes, given the degree of monopoly, are therefore due to changes in unit prime costs—either in the cost of labor or in the cost of materials—and serve the purpose of maintaining a firm's gross profit margin.

Banks, like nonbank firms, are in business to make a profit. The industry itself is dominated by a few large banks of national and international character. Their business is also to produce a product—financial services—which incurs certain costs. They are, however, oligopolistic price setters in "retail" markets while being quantity takers in competitive "wholesale" financial markets. And unlike the case for nonbank firms, the wages of labor are included in fixed costs. The "raw materials" component therefore dominates prime costs. The raw materials, or inputs, of a bank are the deposits it is able to attract and its ability to borrow funds—both of which are the necessary ingredients for its final product, loans. Both have costs attached to them: the interest paid on deposits and the interest paid by banks on borrowed funds. And both are determined in highly competitive markets, although attempts are being made to reduce the uncertainty attached to these "raw materials" costs through forward contracting, e.g., non-negotiable CDs (Certificates of Deposits) of various maturities at stated interest rates and severe penalties for violating the terms of the CD instruments. Other costs include required reserves banks must hold against their deposits and the insurance fees levied against such deposits by the Federal Deposit Insurance Corporation (FDIC).

The revenues of a bank are largely derived from the "prices" charged against bank loans, or the pattern of interest rates, and the interest income from their holdings of short-term investments (Treasury bills—TBs). The interest rates, or prices, of loans are determined by a markup over the "cost of funds" determined by the degree of monopoly or the profit margin of the bank. The equivalent of "excess capacity" in the banking system can be viewed as the excess reserves banks hold and their holdings of such secondary reserves as highly liquid TBs—which can be quickly converted to loan assets virtually on demand either by refusing the Treasury's rollover, or in secondary markets of considerable "depth, breadth, and resiliency." Planned excess capacity in the case of banks, however, would seem to play a lesser role than in the case of nonbank firms to the extent that banks, generally, keep excess reserves at a minimum. This is a general picture that needs now to be fleshed out with a more detailed explanation of the various price-determining components of the banking system.

The lending rates of banks are based on the "cost of funds" and the "interest rate spread" needed to achieve a bank's profit goals. The interest rate spread is simply the margin, or markup, between bank costs and what banks charge for their loans. A rough measure of the spread can be made by comparing the "prime rate"—an administered "price" set by banks supposedly for their best customers—and the Federal Funds rate, which can be taken as a proxy for the cost of funds. Up to the Volcker policy shift of October 1979, the Federal Funds rate was a policy target of the central bank; after that it was free to find its own market level with the central bank concentrating on keeping a variety of monetary aggregates within certain defined upper and lower limits. Federal funds consist of very short term interbank borrowings of excess reserves. Table 3.1 lists the prime rate and the Federal Funds rate from 1955 to 1984. The last column gives the PR/FF ratio, or the prime rate as a markup over the Federal Funds rate. As can be seen more clearly in Figures 3.4 and 3.5, there was some variability in the markup during the immediate postwar years of 1955 to 1964. It was less variable and at a lower overall level between 1966 and 1973, followed by a sharp rise during the 1973–76 OPEC crisis. From 1978 to 1981 the markup ratio remained virtually constant, with a rise in 1982–84 as banks increased their gross profit margin to offset an increase in problematic domestic loans and loans to Third World countries. For example, the percentage of problem loans to total loans outstanding for the largest bank in the United States, the Bank of America, rose from 0.69 percent in 1978 to 4.50 percent in 1982. At other large banks, the

Table 3.1

Markup of the prime rate over the Federal Funds rate (1955–1984)

Year		Prime rate	Federal Funds rate	Markup ratio
1955		3.16	1.78	1.78
1956		3.77	2.73	1.38
1957	(P)	4.20	3.11	1.35
1958	(T)	3.83	1.57	2.44
1959		4.48	3.30	1.36
1960	(P)	4.82	3.22	1.50
1961	(T)	4.50	1.96	2.30
1962		4.50	2.68	1.68
1963		4.50	3.18	1.42
1964		4.50	3.50	1.29
1965		4.54	4.07	1.12
1966		5.63	5.11	1.10
1967		5.61	4.22	1.33
1968		6.30	5.66	1.11
1969	(P)	7.96	8.20	0.97
1970	(T)	7.91	7.18	1.10
1971		5.72	4.66	1.23
1972		5.25	4.43	1.19
1973	(P)	8.03	8.73	0.92
1974		10.81	10.50	1.03
1975	(T)	7.86	5.82	1.35
1976		6.84	5.04	1.36
1977		6.83	5.54	1.23
1978		9.06	7.93	1.14
1979	[V]	12.67	11.19	1.13
1980	(PT)	15.27	13.36	1.14
1981	(P)	18.87	16.38	1.15
1982	(T)	14.86	12.26	1.21
1983		10.79	9.09	1.19
1984		12.04	10.23	1.18

Key: (P) = National Bureau of Economic Research (NBER) cyclical peak, (T) = NBER cyclical trough, [V] = Volcker policy shift of October 1979.
Source: Federal Reserve bulletins, various years.

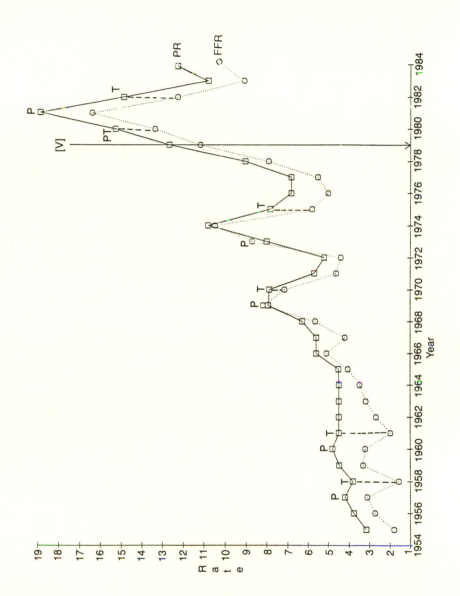

Figure 3.4   Prime rate and Federal Funds rate (yearly data)

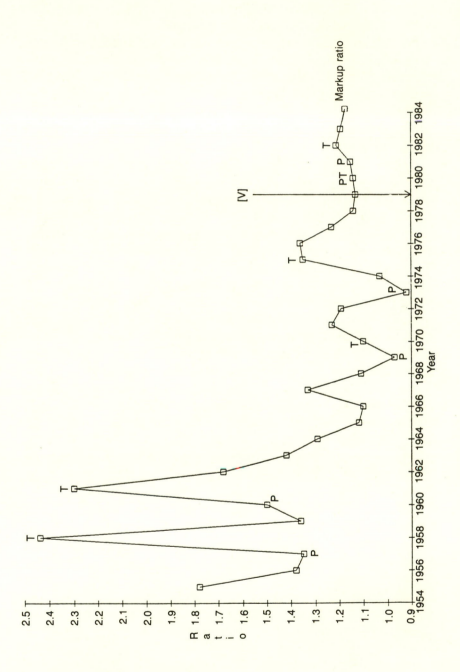

Figure 3.5   PR/FFR markup ratio

percentage rose, for the same time period, from 0.81 percent to 2.56 percent and from 2.1 percent to 5.6 percent.

Part of the explanation for the recent increase in the gross profit margin is to be found in the Depository Institutions Deregulation and Monetary Control Act of 1980, which has increased the amount of interest banks can pay on deposits and has set off a competitive scramble for high interest rate deposits. In the process banks have been forced into making riskier domestic loans at higher interest rates to cover the increased cost of bank funds. Another part of the explanation is the enormous exposure of the larger banks in their loans to Mexico, Brazil, Argentina, and Chile (to mention only the most conspicuous ones) which are in virtual default. For both reasons, if future profit margins were to be threatened by increased domestic and foreign loan defaults banks might well attempt to restore their profit margins by increasing their markup over prime costs. The general increase in k would then be due to bad domestic loans being made under the pressure to reach for higher returns at greater risk to cover the increased costs of funds, and to bad loans to Third World countries. Individual banks, under normal circumstances, are not free to set k at whatever level they wish. Their attempts to maintain k at a level consistent with their desired profit levels are subject to certain constraints. A fall in profits may be the result of outside events that take an individual bank by surprise and over which it has limited control, or of mistakes in the handling of its loan portfolio, or simply of bad management. But the unilateral attempt of an individual bank to restore its profits by raising k may put it so out of line with other banks as to threaten it with a loss of business. When misfortune hits the banking industry as a whole, however, the tendency will be to raise k in order to maintain the profit margin of the industry as a whole.

It is interesting to note from Table 3.1 and its accompanying figures that the markup ratio increases from peak to trough and diminishes as the economy moves toward its next cyclical peak, especially between the years 1955 and 1978. The stickiness of the prime rate and the greater flexibility of the market-determined Federal Funds rate would account for the phenomenon. It would appear, however, that in more recent years banks have learned to adjust their prime rate more synchronously with changes in the Federal Funds rate.

Generally, k can be taken to be relatively stable, at least over the business cycle and, more recently, as a result of a quicker and roughly proportionate response of loan rates to changes in the internal cost of bank funds. Interest rates are therefore determined by a stable markup process over unit prime costs, and changes in interest rates are consequently dependent on changes in unit prime costs, or the cost of funds to banks. According to an excellent summary study of banking practices by Paul Meek of the Federal Reserve Bank of New York,[7] banks mobilize funds for lending purposes by issuing domestic CDs and by paying the needed interest rates in foreign markets to attract Eurodollar deposits. CDs and Eurodollar deposits are in addition to regular deposits and are used by asset-driven commercial banks to expand their loans as a means of achieving their profit objectives. Their measure of the *internal cost of funds*, applied to the domestic loan portfolio, is the 3-month CD rate adjusted upward for reserve requirement costs and the cost of deposit insurance; and for foreign loans, use is made of the London interbank offering rate (LIBOR) for 3-month maturities. These estimates of the internal cost of funds are then applied against the lending and investment operations of a bank.

The next step is to determine the lending rate. Within the major banks the Money Desk is responsible for selling CDs, buying Federal Funds and other sources of borrowed funds—at a cost. The Money Desk is simply the equivalent of a purchasing agent in a nonbank firm, and its "purchases" are made in highly competitive markets. The Asset–Liability Committee (ALCO), on the other hand, is responsible for managing the types and maturities of bank assets and liabilities in keeping with the profit goals of a bank. It is in terms of ALCO decisions that the Money Desk engages in its borrowing operations. ALCO determines the interest rate spread between the bank's overall lending rate and its cost of funds, i.e., it oversees the maintenance of the gross profit margin of the bank.

Fixed lending rates are determined for 60- to 90-day loans in terms of a markup over the *adjusted* CD rate for corresponding maturities. A base rate is set for a bank's most creditworthy customers in keeping with the bank's profit target and then scaled up for other borrowers according to the degree of credit risk involved. Term loans are scaled up from the prime rate for best customers with the cost to the borrower fluctuating with the movements of the prime rate over time. Still other loans, from 30 to 180 days, are set at a markup over the adjusted CD or LIBOR rates for comparable maturities. Although there are a variety of interest rates, depending on the nature, maturity, and risk of different categories of loans and borrowers, they are all determined on a *markup* basis.

The forces affecting the cost of funds in terms of the interest rates paid on deposits were stable under Regulation Q, which set the maximum legal rates payable on different kinds of deposits. Changes in the cost of borrowed funds were therefore attributable to changes of central bank reserve requirements, the discount rate, and the effect of open market operations on the Federal Funds rate. When the CD crisis of the 1960s forced the central bank to allow a series of large increases in the rate payable on negotiable time deposits (Regulation Q), the cost of funds took a sharp leap upward—as did interest rates as a markup over the cost of bank funds. All along, however, Eurodollar CDs were not subject to Regulation Q. And with the passage of the *Depository Institutions Deregulation and Monetary Control Act of 1980*, Regulation Q will have been completely abolished by 1986. This act also authorized thrift institutions to pay higher interest rates on their deposits and to compete with commercial banks by offering checkable deposits. In addition, high paying checking deposits were introduced by the money market and mutual funds of banks and brokerage houses. The cost of funds is in the process of becoming totally uncapped.

Yet another factor in the rise and volatility of bank prime costs was the October 1979 "monetarist" decision of the central bank, under Paul Volcker, to shift from targeting interest rates to targeting the money supply. The shift involved a turn from controlling the Federal Fund rate to an attempt to control nonborrowed bank reserves. As a result, the costs of borrowed funds (the competitively determined "wholesale" interest rates) were left to seek their market-determined levels—in contrast to the "retail" interest rates which make up the "product prices" confronting borrowers as a markup over the "raw material costs" of bankers. These "wholesale" interest rates attained unprecedented heights. The more restrictive actions of the Federal Open Market Committee (FOMC) have therefore had a profound effect on the cost of bank funds, with lending rates following suit on a markup basis. Banks have therefore been forced to achieve their earnings targets by adjusting their lending rates in response to FOMC actions—usually within a week. As the cost of funds in general goes up, the increase is now much more rapidly transmitted to the price of loans. Expectations of future FOMC operations have become a critical factor in ALCO decision making. And with interest rates now becoming a more significant part of the total costs of nonbank firms, prime costs in the nonfinancial sector have increased, leading to a markup of goods prices and, as in 1981–82, to a positive rate of inflation along with massive unemployment.

Given the structural changes that have taken place in the banking industry (in part due to the *Monetary Control Act of 1980*) and the monetarist policies of the central bank, the *base* of the interest structure (as a markup over the "cost of funds") has probably taken a permanent shift upward—even if the central bank should modify its "pragmatic" monetarism and return to a Keynesian policy of targeting interest rates.

More generally, what all this adds up to is that the notion of a market-clearing equilibrium "interest" rate—whether in the old "pro-ductivity-thrift" theory, or the "bastard" Keynesian IS-LM approach, or a market-determined short-run rate—is a theoretical fiction used to provide determinate theoretical solutions within arcane models bearing no relation to the real world. In the universe of economics, interest rates are not the equilibrating force of textbooks. They are essentially a markup over competitive prime costs in a broadly conceived financial sector that is bound to exhibit an even greater concentration of economic power, especially in the banking industry, as the recent, hasty deregulation of the financial sector leads to an even higher level of bank failures, the forced merger of those that do survive with the giants of the banking industry, and the entry into the banking industry of nontraditional types of institutions. In the meantime, the impact of structurally higher and uncapped interest rates all along the liquidity spectrum on what Keynes called the sector of "Industrial Circulation" will be pronounced since interest rates in their varied manifestations will play an even more significant role than before in determining investment, profits, and the process of capital accumulation and growth in a capitalist society.

Notes

1. *A Treatise on Money* (London: Macmillan, 1930), Vol. 1, p. 243, original italics. Subsequent quotations are from Volume 1, Chapters 3 and 15.

2. "The General Theory of Employment," *Quarterly Journal of Economics*, February 1937, "Alternative Theories of the Rate of Interest," *Economic Journal*, June 1937, and "The 'Ex Ante' Theory of the Rate of Interest," *Economic Journal*, December 1937.

3. Although the basic equations are taken from Davidson's *Money and the Real World*, Chapter 7, they have been significantly altered and the model as a whole is sharply and substantively different from that of Davidson.

4. See especially, J. A. Kregel, "Constraints on the Expansion of Output and Employment: Real or Monetary?" *Journal of Post Keynesian Economics*, Winter 1984–85.

5. See Hyman P. Minsky, *John Maynard Keynes* (New York: Columbia University Press, 1975), Chs. 2 and 3.

6. Michal Kalecki, *Selected Essays on the Dynamics of the Capitalist Economy, 1939-1970* (New York: Cambridge University Press, 1971), Ch. 5.

7. Paul Meek, *U.S. Monetary Policy and Financial Markets* (New York: Federal Reserve Bank of New York, 1982), pp. 11, 22, and especially pages 44–51 of Chapter 3 on "Commercial Banks—Managers of Risk."

CHAPTER 4

The endogenous money supply

The money–income link

One of the enigmas of our time is why the quantity theory of money, in one form of another, has survived as long as it has. Nicholas Kaldor regards its current "monetarist" guise as a "terrible curse" and "a visitation of evil spirits" which has caused misery and agony in the form of mass unemployment in the major countries of the West. It is decadent in the Nietzschean sense of going intuitively "for the bad solutions for getting out of difficult situations" while failing "to pick out the good ones."[1] For Kaldor, the rise of monetarism is not due to its "scientific" merits, for it has none. It was the use of monetarism to justify the reactionary shift in the balance of power from labor to capital—at least in Britain and the United States in recent times, and in Chile one might add—that explains its current success in the field of reigning ideas.

True as that may be, the longer-run appeal of the quantity theory of money and its remarkable tenacity lies in its simplistic elegance and its focus on the concept of *money*. The stability of the income velocity of money is one of the key concepts of the quantity theory of money. If, as monetarists insist, it is the functional form of velocity that is stable— which is another way of arguing that the demand for money is stable— then its very stability provides a dependable and rigid *link* between the money stock and the flow of nominal income. And if the income flow corresponds to full utilization of capacity at full employment (the natural unemployment rate), then the money supply is reliably linked to the price level and the rate of inflation, and the old, long-run equipro-portionality requirement of the standard quantity theory of money comes once again into play.

It is this link between the money supply and the levels of income and price (in the short and long runs, respectively) that generates a fear. "People" are not to be trusted with money and its generation, particularly those few who run governments. For the welfare of all, it is argued, money must be isolated and protected from politicians who in the past have either debased it or run it off madly at the printing presses. Control over the money supply must therefore be entrusted to some independent central institution run by professionals (bankers, businessmen, economists, and others with a financial background) who are set apart and immunized from the electoral process—though captives, nonetheless, of some underlying theory which dictates the canons of proper monetary action: either they exercise the independent judgments of discretionary policy, within the confining limits of the theory they subscribe to, or they follow the rigid monetarist rule of mechanically setting the growth rate of the money supply equal to the adjusted long-term growth path of the economy.

It is the futility of trying to control a money supply seen as an exogenous entity that has contributed to the debacle of postwar economic policy and the struggle between neoclassical Keynesians and monetarists. Both the discretionary use of monetary policy (favored by neoclassical Keynesians) and the mechanical application of a monetary rule (championed by Milton Friedman and his followers) share a common assumption—that the money supply is *exogenously* determined. Where they differ is in their respective interpretations of the quantity theory of money and the strength of the link between the money supply and the level of nominal income.

Quantity theorists introduce a causal arrow *from M to Y* which establishes a firm link between the two. In the long run, with real output at its natural full-employment rate, the general price level is found to be uniquely dependent on the supply of money. Neoclassical Keynesians, on the other hand, do not deny that there is a link between *M* and *Y*. To an extent, they accept the causal arrow of the quantity theory of money. Money matters, as the saying goes. What they deny, however, is that the economy tends naturally toward a long-run full-employment equilibrium, or that the rate of turnover of the money supply is a stable function of real income per capita and independent of the rate of interest. With a variable income velocity of money (in response to changes in the rate of interest, as neoclassical Keynesians view it), the link between the money supply and nominal income is tenuous and unpredictable and has little to do, directly, with the level of real output and employment in the real world. Another disagreement between the two camps is that the monetarists assume a direct transmission mechanism from the monetary to the real sector of the economy via the real-balance effect, while neoclassical Keynesians argue in favor of an indirect transmission mechanism operating through the interest-rate effect on investment and hence, through the multiplier, on the real sector of the economy.

Whatever their differences, they both agree that the money supply is exogenously determined by the central bank. For monetarism, given the variable lags of monetary policy and the inability to know where at any moment we are on the business cycle, discretionary attempts by the central bank to manage the money supply contracyclically end up being invariably perverse. The best bet is to ignore short-run problems and to set the growth rate of the money supply equal to the long-term natural growth rate of the economy adjusted for the secular decline in the income velocity of money (with the concept of money more broadly defined than in the case of neoclassical Keynesian economics). Neoclassical Keynesians, operating within their neoclassical synthesis, are convinced that discretionary monetary policy can be successfully combined with an appropriate fiscal policy to fine-tune the economy to a full employment level with relative price stability—Samuelson's artificial restoration of Say's law through the "skillful use of fiscal and monetary policy."

It was the failure of neoclassical Keynesianism, in its attempt to use discretionary economic policy within the standard format of an exogenous money supply, that accounts for the triumph of monetarism—not Kaldor's shift in the balance of power between capital and labor. And it is the understanding of this failure, within the Post Keynesian framework of an *endogenous* money supply, that will define the policies needed to cope with the instability of modern capitalism. This, however, is the subject matter of Chapter 6. For now, we confine the analysis to the origins and the Post Keynesian development of the theory of an endogenous money supply.

The income–money link

Contemporary Post Keynesian monetary economics argues, contrary to the conventional exposition to be found in every elementary money and banking textbook, that the causal arrow flows from the asset side of a bank's balance sheet to its liability side, i.e., banks first grant credit and in doing so they automatically set up demand deposits on the right-hand side of the balance sheet. The argument goes further in maintaining that there is virtually *no* constraint on the ability of banks to issue credit. Reserves are provided, as a matter of course, by the central bank in its capacity as lender of last resort. In addition, the argument of unused overdraft facilities is brought in and although Keynes found it difficult to determine the aggregate amount, and even doubted that banks themselves knew the magnitudes involved, American Post Keynesians have not been similarly discomfitted. They have estimated overdraft facilities as being greater than the M1 supply of money, i.e., over $500 billion. But this begs Keynes's caveat concerning "the extent that the overdraft system is employed and unused overdrafts ignored by the banking system."[2] Mention should also be made of Keynes's view in the *Treatise* that overdraft facilities were neither automatic nor unlimited. Nor does it follow that, to the degree that unused overdrafts exist, they exist where they are most needed, or that they can be instantaneously transferred to those points of need. It is quite possible that a great part of unused overdrafts may remain just that—*unused*. Also, Keynes himself was quite aware that "overdraft facilities may play a lesser part in America in economising the holding of cash."

Many Post Keynesian "monetarists" regard the money supply as a function of the wage rate. An increase in wages forces business into the banks for their increased working capital needs—which, it is argued, are automatically granted by the banks with the full support of the central bank. In effect, the argument is that for any given interest rate level (which the central bank *can* determine through its open market operations) the supply of money is infinitely elastic, i.e., a horizontal curve with respect to the given rate of interest.[3]

The endogeneity models of Sidney Weintraub and Nicholas Kaldor are taken up in the next chapter. The idea of an endogenous money supply, however, is not quite the postwar "discovery" it is sometimes made out to be. In less rigorous form, and lurking somewhere in the background to which it had been assigned, the "banking principle" supported the notion of the money supply spontaneously accommodating "the needs of trade" via a passive financial structure—as opposed to the dominant "currency school," which was based on the "real bills" tradition and which viewed money wages as an endogenous variable determined by demand and supply in competitive labor markets.

An explicitly stated endogeneity principle requires the *full* repudiation of the key precepts of the quantity theory of money, namely, that
the economy naturally tends to full employment, that the velocity of
circulation is stable, and that the causal arrows runs *from* the money
supply *to* nominal income and the price level. Although Keynes satisfied the first two requirements, he was murky on the issue of the causal
arrow. He had not fully emancipated himself from the quantity theory
of money; vestigial traces remained. His position that velocity re-
sponded to changes in the rate of interest led him to deny that the link
between money and nominal income or the price level was stable. He
did not, however, regard the money supply as endogenous. For Keynes
the money supply was exogenously "determined by the action of the
central bank."[4]

As an exogenist, he did not deny that a link existed between M and Y.
What he rejected, unlike contemporary monetarists, was the strength
and stability of that link. Keynes, in other words, never fully broke with
the quantity theory of money. He did not reverse the causal arrow, a
move which is, or ought to be, an absolute requirement for the theory of
an endogenous money supply.[5]

Gunnar Myrdal, on the other hand, was among the first to revive the
"Banking Principle" and to reverse the causal arrow explicitly.[6] Money, to Myrdal, was not to be taken as a *numèraire* in a barter economy.
In a non-barter credit economy money is not "produced" as are non-
monetary goods. It has no conventional supply curve and its "cost" of
production is negligible. The price level in a monetary economy, moreover, cannot be related in some simple, mechanical way to the means of
payment *"because the velocity of circulation of the means of payment
. . . cannot be regarded as constant during a dynamic process"* (p. 14,
italics supplied). Changes in V, for whatever reason, therefore serve to
weaken the link between M and Y as well as between M and P (as
Keynes himself had argued). Myrdal, however, took the argument
much further by arguing explicitly that the link itself should be reversed
with the causal arrow now running *from P* (or Y) *to M* (which Keynes
did not argue). The dominance of the banking principle over the currency school was clearly stated by Myrdal in terms of the price level:

> [T]he quite complicated quantitative relation between the amount of
> means of payment and the "price level" is by no means such that it can be
> said that the amount of means of payment *determines* the price level,
> rather than the other way around. The bankers who are in closest contact

with the "amount of means of payment" have always asserted that the causation is the other way, that the amount of means of payment only reflects obediently the needs of economic life for means of exchange, while it can be said that the demand for means of payment itself depends upon the height of the price level and its tendencies to change . . . [B]ankers . . . were right in denying the "one way" causal connexion *from* the amount of means of payment *to* the "price level." For the changes in the price level and in the amount of means of payment are both simultaneously dependent upon *factors which lie outside the mechanism of payment proper.* (Pp. 14–15, italics supplied)

For Myrdal credit contracts in time were central to any theory of the price level since "credit forms the bulk of all means of payment—*or, at least, determined the velocity of circulation*" (p. 16, italics supplied). By arguing that increases in the demand for money triggered accommodating responses in the money supply which, if not fully adequate, resulted in an increase in what can perhaps be called the "indirect" money supply (i.e., the base period money supply times the percentage change in velocity or the monetary equivalent of a given velocity change which serves to fill the gap, in full or in part), Myrdal was clearly posing the *interdependence* of the demand and supply functions of money and therefore denying the exogeneity of the latter.

The Radcliffe general liquidity thesis

The next major raising of the endogeneity issue came in 1959 when the British Radcliffe Committee issued its controversial Report on *The Working of the Monetary System.*[7] The report cast serious doubt on the effectiveness of monetary policy within the neoclassical synthesis of "Keynesianism without tears."

The main concern of the Radcliffe Committee was to discover how recent changes in the underlying structure "had modified the ability of the authorities to influence the [economic] system by monetary methods" (p. 3). For any meaningful evaluation of monetary policy, changes in the structure of financial institutions had to be taken into account as they occurred over historical time. And the aims of monetary policy, and the techniques used to achieve them, were "all conditioned by the facts of the economic situation *and the ideas of the time*" (p. 6, italics supplied). Their overall conclusion was that the money supply had become largely irrelevant and that an effective monetary policy could be achieved only by control over the general liquidity of the economy—the Radcliffe *liquidity thesis*.

The dependence of traditional monetary policy on what the committee called *the interest-incentive effect*, or the attempt of the monetary
authorities to influence the level of aggregate demand through the
impact of interest-rate changes on the "incentive to purchase capital
goods" (p. 130), was rejected. The idea of an interest rate operating on
the demand side as a cost to borrowers was found to be virtually
nonexistent. "We have sought, without much success," wrote the
committee about the interest-incentive effect, "for convincing evidence of its presence in recent years" (p. 131).[8] The committee then
turned to its major finding, *the general liquidity effect*:

> [T]he monetary authorities can bring about a change in the liquidity
> condition of financial institutions and of business firms and people gener-
> ally, so that those wanting money to spend (whether for capital develop-
> ment or other purposes) find it more (or less) difficult to get than before.
> (Pp. 130–131)

If the interest-rate effect on the demand side, within its institutionally
feasible range, can be swamped by the profit expectations of businessmen, the only way to abort the demand for money is through severe
restrictions on the availability of credit. As the committee noted, "[I]f
the money for financing the project cannot be got on any tolerable terms
at all, *that is the end of the matter*" (p. 131, italics supplied). But
restricting the availability of credit implies more than just restricting
the money supply, which is only a *part* of the general liquidity of the
economy. "It is the whole liquidity position that is relevant to spending
decisions" not just the money supply, for "decisions to spend on goods
and services—the decisions that determine the level of demand—are
influenced by the liquidity of spenders" as well as by "the liquidity of
the various groups of financial institutions" (p. 132). In other words,
account must be taken not only of the income, the convertible assets,
and the borrowing power of spenders, but also of "the methods, moods
and resources of financial institutions and other firms which are prepared (on terms) to finance other people's spending" (p. 132). The
Radcliffe Committee then went on to hammer home its point on the
irrelevance of the money supply as the object of monetary control:

> [S]pending is not limited by the amount of money in existence; . . . it is
> related to the amount of money people think they can get hold of, whether

by receipts of income (for instance from sales), by disposal of capital assets or by borrowing . . . *[S]pending is not limited by the amount of money in existence [as can be seen] by reference to the velocity of circulation.* (P. 133, italics supplied)

If the conventional money supply is restricted or held constant and the level of spending, nevertheless, continues to increase—as it is wont to do—this can only mean that the velocity of circulation has gone up. Within traditional monetary theory, of the Keynesian variety, there is supposed to be some outer limit to velocity, for when all idle balances have been activated and transactions balances have been pared to the bone in response to excessively high interest rates, then velocity will have reached its *theoretical* maximum and nominal GNP would have to grind to a halt—at which point conventional monetary policy would hold.[9] This, of course, assumes a stable financial framework, which, in turn, implies the total absence of financial innovations. Apart from the problem of closing the barn door too late, the existence of a velocity maximum can itself be challenged, as indeed the Radcliffe Committee did. "*[W]e cannot find,*" wrote the Committee, *"any reason for supposing, or any experience in monetary history indicating, that there is any limit to the velocity of circulation of money"* (p. 133, italics supplied).[10] This was the most important statement in the entire report, the full implication of which the committee failed to grasp.

Trapped within its own traditional way of looking at the demand for money, the committee was reluctant to make "more use of this concept" on the grounds that velocity "is a statistical concept that tells us nothing of the motivation that influences the level of demand. An analysis of liquidity, on the other hand, directs attention to the behavior and decisions that do directly influence the level of demand" (p. 133). Or, as Keynes put it in the *General Theory* (p. 299): "[T]he 'income-velocity of money' is, in itself, merely a name which explains nothing. There is no reason to expect that it will be constant. For it depends . . . on many complex and variable factors. The use of the term . . . has led to nothing but confusion." The committee, in effect, chose to remain within the Cambridge tradition, which emphasizes k, or the money–income ratio, over its reciprocal, V. The difference is between "money sitting" and "money on the wing," to use D. H. Robertson's distinction. The Cambridge tradition prefers "money sitting" because it leads directly to the psychological motives for holding money—with its emphasis on the *demand* for money—as compared to the mechanical barreling of the money *supply* through the economy in the form of Irving Fisher's *V*. Although "liquidity," as used by the committee, is identical to "velocity," the committee's failure to follow up on the explicit use of *V* was unfortunate, since the concept of velocity focuses attention more directly on the impact of financial innovations—a more important phenomenon *on the supply side* (which turned out to be the committee's main concern in the report) than the demand-side "motives" for holding money. Events subsequent to the report make it even more important to return to the concept of velocity, especially in the current situation.

If a velocity maximum is the outer limit of a movement *along* an increasingly steep $V(i)$ function, then the absence of such a maximum must imply a series of parametric *shifts* of the $V(i)$ curve to the right—which is another way of talking about the impact of financial innovations on the level of general liquidity in the economy. In these terms, the shambles of conventional monetary policy becomes transparent.[11] From the Radcliffe Committee's point of view, emphasis was therefore to be placed "on all those groups of institutions whose behavior seems to bear in an important degree on the amount of liquidity, rather than just the amount of money, in the economy" (p. 133). Financial innovations and control over the velocity changes they induce are the critical factor for any effective monetary policy—one that goes considerably beyond an attempt to control the credit-creating function of the commercial banking system. It was clear to the Radcliffe Committee that "the more efficient the financial structure, the more can the velocity of circulation be stretched without serious inconvenience being caused" (p. 133).

What the Radcliffe Committee had argued, although not saying so explicitly, was that the money supply was *endogenous*, and being so not subject to control by the monetary authorities. Indeed, as will be seen, the central bank was itself largely responsible for the endogeneity of the money supply. The Radcliffe liquidity thesis, therefore, represented the complete repudiation of a conventionally conceived monetary policy acting on a presumably exogenous money supply.

Notes

1. Kaldor, *Origins of the New Monetarism*, p. 3.
2. "The 'Ex Ante' Theory of the Rate of Interest." See also Keynes, *A Treatise on Money*, Vol. 1, pp. 41 and 236.
3. See, in particular, Basil Moore, "Wages, Bank Lending, and the Endogeneity

of Credit Money," in Marc Jarsulic, ed., *Money and Macro Policy* (Boston: Kluwer-Nijhoff Publishing, 1985); see also his references to his four other works on the subject. For an excellent overview of the "mainline" Post Keynesian position, see Marc Lavoie, "Credit and Money: The Dynamic Circuit, Overdraft Economics, and Post-Keynesian Economics," in Jarsulic, *Money and Macro Policy*, and "The Endogenous Flow of Credit and the Post-Keynesian Theory of Money" (May 1983, unpublished).

4. *The General Theory*, p. 247.

5. The closest he came to doing so can be found on page 305 of the *General Theory*: "I would repeat the warning . . . as to what variables are taken as independent . . . [T]he extreme complexity of the relationship between prices and the quantity theory of money [is exhibited] when we attempt to express [the relationship] in a formal manner."

6. Gunnar Myrdal, *Monetary Equilibrium* (London: William Hodge & Co. Ltd., 1939). This is a fascinating book in many respects as well as an amusingly self-satisfied one. Myrdal is cross that English speaking economists paid no attention to the teachings of Knut Wicksell. He complains that Denis Robertson in his *Banking Policy and the Price Level* "obviously lacks a thorough knowledge of the content of the monetary studies of Wicksell and his pupils and he has therefore been forced unnecessarily to think for himself," and he dismisses, as well, Keynes in his *Treatise* on the ground that he "too suffers from the attractive Anglo-Saxon kind of unnecessary originality" (p. 8). The Swedes, apparently, had said it all before, or so Myrdal thought.

7. *Committee on the Working of the Monetary System: Report* (London: Her Majesty's Stationery Office, August 1959).

8. Substantial support for the committee's finding is to be found in the *Committee on the Working of the Monetary System: Principal Memoranda of Evidence* (Vol. 3, Part 13, Her Majesty's Stationery Office, 1959). This finding, however, holds for *the institutionally feasible range of interest-rate variation*, that is, between the interest-rate floor and a conventionally held interest-rate ceiling. Given the relatively narrow range of interest rates in the recent past, interest-rate considerations (as a cost to borrowers) could be easily swamped by the profit expectations of businessmen during boom periods. It is only with the October 1979 policy shift of Paul Volcker in the United States, and its equivalent in Britain under the Thatcher government, that interest rates have been uncapped. In these new circumstances, the extraordinary level of interest rates, acting on the demand side, would seem to have given a new life to the interest rate as a cost to borrowers, or, in Radcliffe terms, *the interest-incentive effect*.

9. For a more detailed discussion of the theoretical velocity maximum, see Chapter 3 above.

10. The following two exchanges from the *Minutes of Evidence* of the Radcliffe Committee are of special interest. The first took place on October 24, 1957, between Professors A. K. Cairncross and R. S. Sayers, both members of the Radcliffe Committee, and Sir Robert Hall, Economic Adviser to H. M. Government and Director, Economic Section, H. M. Treasury (p. 111):

> *Professor Cairncross*: [T] supply of money in terms of bank deposits has not varied very much over the past five or six years; and yet the level of prices has risen very appreciably?
> *Sir Robert Hall*: Yes. I think we call attention to the changes which can take place in the desire to hold liquid balances.
> *Professor Cairncross*: Do you have any views as to the limit? Do you believe the economy might be run in fact on a very small sum of money in relation to what exists now? Where do you get to the point where you think liquidity is about right?

Sir Robert Hall: It is a function of the rate of interest, to our way of thinking. We also think that there is not, except in quite abnormal circumstances, an indefinite extensibility of the active supply of money at the expense of the inactive. At any time there are minimum balances which every individual or corporation will wish to hold, and he will find serious inconvenience if he lets them drop below that level. We feel that you get down somewhere or other to some level which you must have on the average, because it is so inconvenient to have to realise an asset if you happen to want money.

Professor Sayers: This irreducible level will depend in part on the availability of other highly liquid assets, or what we might call near-money. Has not the increasing availability over the last half century of these highly liquid assets made it possible for the national income to expand relatively to the supply of money quite considerably, without any appreciable rise being thereby engendered in the rate of interest, such as one would expect to see?

Sir Robert Hall: Yes.

The following exchange took place the next day between Lord Radcliffe, the Chairman of the Committee, and H. C. Mynors, Deputy Governor of the Bank of England (p. 137):

Lord Radcliffe: Would you think that the degree of liquidity required in the kind of conditions we are living in today is highly compressible or elastic, or fairly fixed? We have seen in the last few years how the country has gone along with a good deal less money relative to income than it used to have. Do you think this is a process which could go on almost indefinitely?

Mr. Mynors: Could we think about that, Mr. Chairman? That is not a question that we should like to tackle offhand.

Lord Radcliffe: We should be grateful if you would. I think the question is: assuming that an important element in this situation has been the increased velocity in the use of money, is there a point at which you can foresee that expansion of velocity being exhausted?

I am grateful to Nancy J. Wulwick of LeMoyne College for having brought these passages to my attention.

11. This would be shown in Figure 3.3 as a series of rightward parametric shifts of the $V(i)$ curve in response to a sequence of money supply reductions yielding, in the process, a step-function for the velocity curve as a result of financial innovations. For two early expositions of this argument, see Hyman P. Minsky, "Central Banking and Money Market Changes," *Quarterly Journal of Economics*, May 1957, reprinted in Minsky, *Can "It" Happen Again?*, and Stephen W. Rousseas, "Velocity Changes and the Effectiveness of Monetary Policy, 1951–57," *Review of Economics and Statistics*, February 1960; also Peter L. Bernstein, "The Response of Income Velocity to Interest Rate Changes: A Comment," and Stephen W. Rousseas, "Rejoinder," *Review of Economics and Statistics*, November 1960. For a three-dimensional representation of velocity shifts and their relation to GNP, see Stephen W. Rousseas, *Monetary Theory* (New York: Random House, 1972), pp. 110–115, 124–128. A classic historical study of velocity is that of George Garvy and Martin R. Bly, *The Velocity of Money* (New York: Federal Reserve Bank of New York, 1969). For a more recent and surprising discussion of the problem of financial innovations from the former president of the Federal Reserve Bank of New York, see Anthony M. Solomon, "Financial Innovation and Monetary Policy" (Remarks Before the Joint Luncheon of the American Economic and American Finance Associations, December 28, 1981, Washington, D.C.), reprinted by the Federal Reserve Bank of New York, 1982.

CHAPTER 5

The Weintraub–Kaldor models of endogeneity

The Weintraub model of endogeneity

A full-fledged theory of an endogenous money supply requires an outright rejection of the quantity theory of money in three clear-cut ways: (1) rejection of the notion that a capitalist economy naturally tends toward a long-run, full-employment equilibrium; (2) rejection of the argument that the income velocity of money is stable and independent of the rate of interest (or, in more contemporary terms, that the demand for money is a stable function of real income per capita); and, most important of all, (3) rejection of the quantity theory's causal arrow running *from* the money supply *to* either nominal income or the general price level. These points were made in Chapter 4. Put in more positive terms, for purposes of this chapter, the theory of an endogenous money supply, in its most extreme form, argues: (1) that capitalism is inherently unstable; (2) that the underlying financial structure is given to waves of financial innovations in response to the conventional tight-money policies of the central bank; and (3) that any increase in nominal income causes an increase in the supply of money sufficient to accommodate the resulting increase in the demand for money.

There is ample historical evidence for the first two positively stated propositions—that capitalism is inherently unstable and subject, periodically, to waves of financial innovation; although most Post Keynesians tend to ignore the latter. It is the third proposition concerning the *full* accommodation of changes in the demand for money that is debatable and in need of careful elaboration. The critical question is whether the supply of money *fully* and *automatically* accommodates any increase in the demand for it, or whether it does so only partially, with changes in the income velocity of money making up a part or all of the shortfall. If the former is the case, as indeed some Post Keynesian "monetarists" believe it to be, then the theory of an endogenous money supply implies its own version of Say's law as applied, in reverse, to the monetary sector, namely, that *demand creates its own supply*. If the latter is the case, the argument is more complicated but less simple-minded and less subject to controversy—while attaining essentially the same results, although posing at the same time a critical problem for the continued viability of capitalism that the proponents of Say's law in reverse avoid by recourse to their own Post Keynesian version of the neoclassical fine-tuning hypothesis.

One model for an endogenous money supply is that of Sidney Weintraub.[1] Weintraub bases his case for the endogeneity of the money supply on his well-known *wage theorem*: that, on the whole, prices are determined by some markup over unit labor costs, i.e.,

$$P = k \left(\frac{W}{Q} \right)$$

where k is the given degree of monopoly in the economy determined by the exogenous institutional environment within which each firm operates,[2] and the ratio of the total nominal wage bill (W) to the level of real output (Q) is a measure of the *unit labor cost* of producing that total output. By dividing W and Q by L (the total labor input), we see that the equation becomes:

$$P = k \left(\frac{w}{A} \right)$$

where w is the average annual wage rate in nominal terms, and A the average productivity of employed labor (Q/L), which is assumed to grow at a relatively constant rate over time. If the relative increase in the nominal wage rate exceeds that of the average productivity of labor ($\dot{w} > \dot{A}$), prices will rise. In general terms, therefore, we can write:

$$P = P(w)$$

where w is *exogenously* determined by the process of collective bargaining. In short, *prices are a function of nominal wages*, positively related—a major tenet of American Post Keynesian economics.

Weintraub's argument on the endogeneity of money follows directly from his wage theorem in a model that takes the income velocity of money as given. Any excessive increase in the wage rate ($\dot{w} > \dot{A}$) will cause prices to rise by some predetermined and stable markup over unit labor costs. The immediate effect, for any given level of real output (Q) and its corresponding level of employment, is a proportionate increase in nominal income (Y). The argument is simple enough. Since nominal income is the general price level times real output ($Y = PQ$), then given Q it follows that the causal arrow runs from wages to prices to nominal income, with nominal income increasing in direct proportion to the increase in prices in the immediate short run.

The increase in nominal income, due to a rise in unit labor costs, results in an increased transactions demand for money (credit) for any given level of real output. Therefore, *if real output and employment are to be maintained*, the supply of money will have to increase. The question is how and by how much—in a fully accommodating fashion or only partially? If, as Weintraub assumes, the velocity of circulation is constant, a *full* accommodation will be required if real output and employment are to be maintained. If the central bank flatly refuses to increase the money supply, then the resulting excess demand for money will cause interest rates to rise with the expected Keynesian result of a fall in investment leading, via the multiplier effect, to a decrease in real output and employment—thus bringing about a forced equality in the demand and supply of money via a *decrease* in the demand for money at the lower level of real output (itself a consequence of the central bank's refusal to increase the money supply). The adjustment comes about by a fall in real output and employment, thus washing out the increased demand for money by restoring nominal income to its original level.

The same analysis applies to any increase in the money supply that is less than fully accommodating. Real output and employment will still fall, although by less than in the case of no accommodation at all. In either event, the failure of accommodation (none or only partial, *with V constant*) results in a higher price level *and* a lower level of output and employment—which emerges as Weintraub's explanation of the phenomenon of *stagflation*. Stagflation, in this case, follows from Weintraub's wage theorem plus the actions of a recalcitrant central bank.

What is troubling about the negative implications of the model is that it is *assumed* that the central bank has the power to prevent an increase in the money supply, or to determine the limited amount by which it will be allowed to increase. That the central bank appears to be able to do so follows from the critical assumption of the model that the income velocity of money is constant, thus reestablishing the traditional link between M and Y based on the highly doubtful view that the money supply is exogenous and controllable. Any theory of the endogeneity of the money supply, it would seem, should be able to argue (as does Myrdal) that the money supply will increase no matter what the wishes of the monetary authorities happen to be; that is, that the central bank cannot control the supply of money. This is not possible within the Weintraub model (as specified) since it would require an explicit admission of a variable income velocity of money into the analysis. With velocity assumed to be constant, Weintraub argues that any increase in demand associated with an increase in nominal income will be *fully* accommodated by the actions of the central bank. This argument for complete endogeneity, however, is based on *political*, not economic, considerations. For example, if the policy goal of the government is to *sustain* the levels of real output and employment, then this can be done (given V) only if there is a full accommodation by the central bank of the increased demand for money. Automatic, full accommodation also explains why velocity is a constant. With the money supply increasing in proportion to all increases in nominal income, the income–money ratio remains unaffected.

In short, monetary policy, *for any given level of employment*, must serve a ''sustaining function'' by meeting the increased ''needs of trade'' due to an increase in money wages above the productivity of labor. If the political pressures for preventing a fall in employment are strong enough, then the causal link of M to Y is broken by the political instructions to the central bank to accommodate in full any increase in the demand for money; that is, the causal link is reversed by the exercise of political authority. *But in another sense it continues to exist in its original form as an underlying economic phenomenon.* The link lies beneath the surface as a fundamental force. Endogeneity, in effect, becomes a form of closet exogeneity! Money does indeed matter, for if it does not meet the ''needs of trade'' then we revert, on another level, to the old link between M and Y, and real output and employment will fall in the absence of full accommodation—something it is assumed the political system would not tolerate, at least until recent times. The following quotation from Weintraub is of interest:

For the real phenomena of growth and full employment, monetary policy does remain decisive . . . It could regain its former dominance but only if it were allowed to make inroads on money wages at a cost in unemployment and human misery *which would at present be considered unacceptable to modern democratic societies.*[3]

In summary, for Weintraub changes in the price level are the result of changes in unit labor costs, and the money supply is directly linked to the level of real output and employment and only *indirectly* to the price level. The indirect link to the price level is through the tempering of wage demands brought about by the unemployment that would follow a less than full accommodation of the increased demand for money. Essentially, Weintraub argues that, as long as money wages are exogenously determined around the bargaining table, monetary policy has only an indirect link to the price level, and then only if the central bank is able to defy the political authorities to an extreme degree, that is, by causing a *large* fall in real output and employment. Barring that, prices are a function of wages, not the money supply, which has only a "sustaining" role to play. Or, in Weintraub's words:

So long as the price level, for the most part, is set by wage bargains which are beyond the control of the Central Bank, the Monetary Authority, at best, can ensure ample supplies of money to remove financial impediments to full employment and growth. It is ill-equipped . . . to exert any effective control over price levels. (Ibid.)

The impotence of monetary policy, however, is only with respect to any direct link to the price level. Its power, when taken to extremes, to cause unemployment and thus indirectly contain or slow down the rate of inflation is not disputed. Nevertheless, the Weintraub theory of an endogenous money supply is based on the assumption that responsible political leaders will not tolerate a significant lapse from relatively full employment.[4] It has turned out to be a liberal delusion that has been shattered in the United States under President Reagan and in Britain under Margaret Thatcher—not to mention the "socialist" governments of France, Spain, Italy, and Greece and the current or former social democratic governments of Germany and the Scandinavian countries which have undertaken similar policies.[5]

The Kaldor model of endogeneity

A variation on Weintraub's theme can be found in the works of other Post Keynesians.[6] The argument now becomes that of the central bank's primary responsibility to guarantee the solvency of the financial sector. Acting as a lender of last resort through the discount window (the bank rate), the central bank gets hoisted on its own petard. To prevent credit crunches from turning into disastrous debt deflations, the monetary authorities have no choice but to accommodate the "needs of trade." The argument was succinctly put by Nicholas Kaldor:

> [T]he [Central] Bank cannot *refuse* the discounting of "eligible bills" rendered to it . . . If it did, by setting a fixed limit to the amount which the Bank is prepared to discount on a daily or a weekly basis . . . the Bank would fail in its function as "lender of last resort" to the banking system which is essential to ensure that the clearing banks do not become insolvent as a result of a lack of liquidity. Precisely because the monetary authorities cannot afford the disastrous consequences of a collapse of the banking system . . . the "money supply" in a credit-money economy is *en*dogenous, not *ex*ogenous—it varies in direct response to changes in the public "demand" to hold cash and bank deposits and not independently of that demand.[7]

What this amounts to is a *perfectly elastic*, or horizontal, supply curve of money *at any interest-rate level (the discount rate) set and maintained by the central bank*—which means that monetary demand creates its own supply, in full. Nicholas Kaldor pioneered this particular formulation of the theory of an endogenous money supply, one that many Post Keynesians have accepted uncritically.[8] But where Weintraub's theory of endogeneity follows directly from his wage theorem, Kaldor's is solidly based on the "lender-of-last-resort" function of the central bank. It bears emphasizing, however, that compared to the United States the lender of last resort function in England is substantively different. In England it is more directly linked to the PSBR, or Public Sector Borrowing Requirement, i.e., in avoiding the "crowding-out" effect. The Bank of England serves as a lender of last resort largely for the discount houses which are responsible for Treasury bill tenders. The main purpose of the lender-of-last-resort function is not to serve the private financial needs of banks, but to meet the needs of public debt financing. The "political" argument therefore plays a lesser role in Kaldor's formulation than in Weintraub's, although it does not totally disappear from view.

In his earlier 1980 monograph,[9] Kaldor concerned himself with "Friedman's contention . . . that the velocity of circulation, in terms of conventional money, has been relatively stable." In Friedman's formulation, the stability of the velocity function is simply another way of talking about the stability of the demand function for money, thereby placing the emphasis on the exogenous money supply (or the high-powered monetary base) and the problems of coping with it in terms of lags. Kaldor's reply was that, in those historical periods where the velocity of circulation was stable, the *supply* of money was unstable; i.e., as in Weintraub's argument, "an increased demand for money evoked an increase in supply. The money supply 'accommodated itself' to the needs of trade: rising in response to an expansion, and vice versa." Kaldor drove his point home by stating: "The explanation . . . for all the empirical findings on the 'stable money function' is that the 'money supply' is 'endogenous,' not 'exogenous.' " For Kaldor, "the relative stability in the demand for money is a reflection of the instability in its supply; if the supply of money had been kept more stable the velocity of circulation would have been more *un*stable."

Either the monetary authorities in the United States are simply not able to control the level of bank reserves through open market operations or, as in the case of England, banks have complete and unlimited access to the discount window of the central bank. For Kaldor, accommodating changes in the supply of money, in response to increases in the demand for it, reflect the rate of change in money income which in turn depends on a much broader base than Weintraub's solitary wage theorem. It depends on such factors as: (1) the pressure of demand, (2) domestic investment, (3) exports, (4) fiscal policy, (5) the rate of wage inflation, and (6) variations in public sector borrowing requirements.

In the latest (1982) and most rigorous formulation of his theory of the endogeneity of the money supply, Kaldor states the case unequivocally: "*[A]t any time, or at all times, the money stock will be determined by demand, and the rate of interest determined by the Central Bank.*"[10] That is, the money supply is *endogenous* and demand-driven while the rate of interest (the bank rate) is the *exogenously* determined basic price of money set and administered by the central bank. This constitutes a complete reversal of traditional monetary theory. Contrary to neoclassical Keynesians and monetarists, the monetary authorities, in Kaldor's view, have virtually no control over the money supply—which is "dependent on demand, governed by the level of income" and which the central bank must accommodate as lender of last resort if the collapse of the financial system is to be avoided.

For Kaldor, however, it is within the power of the central bank to determine the bank rate unilaterally (in a closed economy). If the bank rate, it could be argued, determines the internal cost of bank funds then it would also determine the loan rates of various categories of bank loans as a markup over the cost of such funds. In the final analysis, interest rates would not be endogenously determined by the interplay of demand and supply in competitive financial markets. The central bank, in other words, would have the power to impose its will on that of the market and set the pattern of interest rates where it wants—presumably at the level consistent with that rate of investment which, via the multiplier-accelerator process, will validate the government's full-employment policy. At any rate, that is one interpretation that can be put on Kaldor's model although he, himself, does not quite put it that way. However it is interpreted, Kaldor is clear on one matter: the interest rate (or pattern of interest rates) "is not a dependent but an independent variable" totally under the control of the central bank, and the purpose of monetary policy is to target the rate of interest, not the stock of money, over which, in any event, it has no control—the stock of money is demand-determined, i.e., all increases in the demand for money are fully accommodated by the central bank acting as lender of last resort.

The demand for money, in short, is a function of nominal income and changes in the demand for money are the result of "changes in the level of production and income" brought about by changes in the rate of interest. The rate of interest, in other words, has no *direct* effect on the "desire to hold money"; it has an *indirect* effect brought about solely by induced changes in the level of income. That is, changes in the rate of interest, brought about by changes in the bank rate, have a *direct* effect on investment and thus on income via the multiplier-accelerator model. The causal scenario runs as follows: a fall in the rate of interest causes an increase in investment which, in turn, causes income to rise by some multiple of the increase in investment. This increase in income results in an increased demand for transactions balances which, at a given bank rate, is met by the central bank acting as a lender of last resort to the banks.

The endogeneity of money, in Kaldor's model, is therefore explained by his insistence that "the Central Bank cannot close the 'discount window' without endangering the solvency of the banking system; they must maintain their function as a 'lender of last resort.' '' Although the central bank could technically seek to restrain or ease credit by changes in the bank rate, it cannot afford to slam the discount window shut without raising the spectre of a financial collapse. For Kaldor changes in the bank rate are intended to affect investment, and the resulting induced changes in the demand for money must be met by the central bank if the overall economic policy targets are not to be negated.

Weintraub's "political" argument for explaining the endogeneity of money has been replaced, by Kaldor, with a money stock that is solidly linked to the lender of last resort function of the central bank. The differences between the two models of endogeneity can perhaps be made clearer by the use of Kaldor's basic (and not too clear) diagram of the endogenous money supply.

A diagrammatic exposition

Figure 5.1 shows the demand for money as a function of the level of nominal income. The negative slope of the curve indicates, as one moves down the $D(Y)$ curve, that the higher the level of nominal income the higher will the demand for money be. It is, in effect, a reversal of the causal arrow which now runs *from Y to M*. If, heroically, we assume (as Kaldor does) a permanent incomes policy firmly in place and operating with full effectiveness, the price level will be a constant and the $D(Y)$ curve will indicate the higher nominal demand for money at each higher level of real output and employment, and conversely. The vertical axis indicates the exogenously determined rate of interest set by the central bank. At each and every possible interest rate there exists a supply of money curve horizontal to the money axis, i.e., the central bank's "lender of last resort" behavior assures a fully endogenous money supply. [11]

We start at the equilibrium intersection point A in Figure 5.1, where the demand for money is exactly equal to its supply at that level of real output corresponding to the interest rate level of i_2. Assume, next, that the indicated real output level does not correspond to a full-employment equilibrium. Assume also that the state of confidence and business expectations is given so that any change in the rate of interest will result in a movement *along* a stable marginal efficiency of capital schedule. The central bank, presumably at the instigation of the elected government in power, reduces the rate of interest to i_1 so as to stimulate

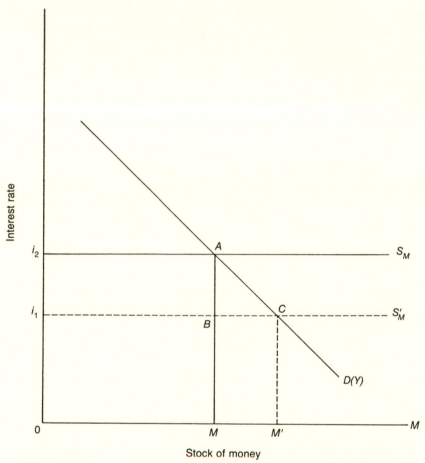

Figure 5.1

real investment in order to bring the economy to its full-employment level of real output. *We discretely overlook the fact that this turns out to be a Post Keynesian version of neoclassical fine tuning!*

With the price level unchanged because of the incomes policy of the government, the increase in real output will cause nominal income to rise. In turn, the rise in nominal income will result in a movement along the $D(Y)$ demand curve from point A to point C, with the demand for money increasing from M to M' on the horizontal axis. As a lender of last resort, the central bank passively allows the money supply to increase by the same amount, BC, so that at point C demand and supply are once again in equilibrium. The movement down the $D(Y)$ curve from point A to point C generates the money supply increase of BC. The supply curve for money is dynamically identical to the $D(Y)$ curve, which is simply another way of saying that demand creates its own supply via the central bank acting as lender of last resort through the discount window or, in the case of the United States, as a result of fully accommodating open market operations. In equilibrium the supply curve of money, at the corresponding interest rate, is infinitely elastic (a horizontal line). The endogeneity of the money supply is thus established by Kaldor.

In summary, the dynamic identity of the supply and demand curves for money, between the points A and C in Figure 5.1, is a consequence, in Kaldor's model, of the fall in the exogenous rate of interest which induces an increase in investment and thus in the level of nominal income leading, in turn, to an increased transactions demand for money—which is passively accommodated by the central bank. But it needs stressing that the response of supply to an increase in demand is *not* spontaneous. It requires the appropriate "sustaining action" (to use Weintraub's phrase) of the central bank. To that extent, Kaldor's model is also predicated on "political" considerations and therefore subject to the same criticism. The inverse of Say's law as applied to the monetary sector is on shaky ground, indeed, at least with respect to *full* accommodation.

Kaldor's diagram can also be used to illustrate the Weintraub model of an endogenous money supply. We begin again at the new equilibrium point A in Figure 5.2, only this time there is no permanent incomes policy in place and the price level is therefore free to change. Assume now that in the wage bargaining process unit labor costs increase ($\dot{w} > \dot{A}$) thus causing an increase in the price level and (given the level of real output) in nominal income. The increase in nominal income (with real output constant) implies a *shift* in the demand curve for money from $D(Y)$ to $D(Y)'$, or by the distance AB. At the initial interest rate i_2, the demand for money will exceed the supply of money by AB, or by the amount of the shift in the $D(Y)$ curve. If the central bank were to drive the interest rate up to i_3, real output would fall by an amount sufficient (at the higher price level) to decrease nominal income to where it was originally, thereby mopping up the excess demand for money. We will, in effect, have moved along the higher $D(Y)'$ curve from point B to point C—with C directly above point A in the case of total non-accommodation and with velocity constant. Nominal income will have reverted to its original value via a decrease in real output as an

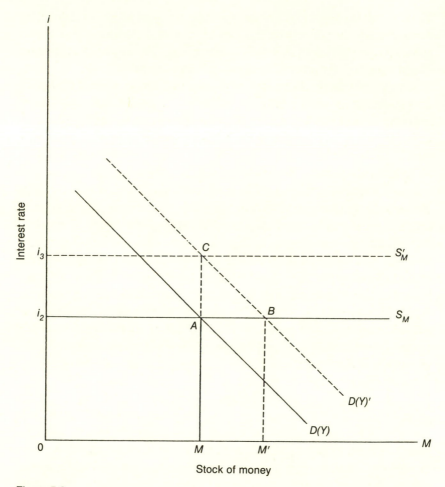

Figure 5.2

offset to the increase in price. With the demand for money back to its original level, demand and supply will once more be in equilibrium at point C. But this is hardly an example of an endogenous money supply. Indeed, it assumes that the money supply is exogenous and fully under the control of the central bank.

Assuming that the resulting *stagflation* would be politically intolerable, the central bank (in Weintraub's model) would be directed to maintain the interest rate at i_2. In the process of doing so (via open market operations in the case of the United States), the level of bank reserves and thus the money supply (assuming banks keep their excess reserves at a minimum) will have increased by AB, thus achieving once more an equality between the demand and supply of money at point B on the higher $D(Y)'$ curve. Again, it is clear that the endogeneity of the money supply is a "political" phenomenon involving "sustaining operations" on the part of a compliant central bank.

It is a highly conjectural argument, one that carries with it the heavy freight of a categorical imperative. The fact is that central bank policy is not and never has been fully accommodating, at least not as a conscious policy objective. If it were, then the velocity function, as Friedman has always claimed, would be stable—though not for the reasons he gave. This particular version of Say's law in reverse results in a constant V because of the central bank's full and automatic accommodation of the conventional money supply to any increase in the demand for money. It implies that M increases in proportion to Y, thereby leaving the income–money ratio unchanged. The velocity of money, however, has not been constant, or even stable in its functional form, and it is important to note that the Weintraub–Kaldor models of Figures 5.1 and 5.2 both assume, in equilibrium, a perfectly elastic, horizontal supply of money curve and thus a constant income velocity of money as a result. In a very *un*-Keynesian way, *it divorces the income velocity of money from changes in the rate of interest.* So do the monetarists, but for totally different reasons.

The velocity component of the endogenous money supply

In a later book, Weintraub pulled back from the notion of full accommodation. "Money supply endogeneity," he wrote, "may not be complete; it has been erratic and only intermittently predictable. Nevertheless, it exists, though the relationship is not readily captured in a tidy analytic model."[12] He went on to argue that predicting the *degree* or extent of accommodation would "require a psychological profile of MA [Monetary Authority] personalities and staff." He could have added all the other participants in the private financial sector as well. Prediction is simply not possible. The degree of accommodation will vary with varying circumstances and pressures—*and with the response of the private financial sector in defiance of the policies pursued by the monetary authorities.*

The argument that the money supply is "demand-determined" and not "supply-determined," in Kaldor, results in a stable velocity function (in contradistinction to the monetarist position) "only because the ease of the response of the money supply to changes in the volume of money transactions makes changes in velocity superfluous . . . [I]f the velocity of circulation *appears* stable it is only because the quantity of money stock is so *unstable* . . . It [is] a mirage.''[13] It is, in other words, only when *full* accommodation takes place that the supply of money curve, at a given rate of interest, is perfectly elastic with velocity a constant as a result. *In the case of Kaldor, the exogenous interest rate coupled with the lender of last resort function of the central bank severs the Keynesian link between velocity and the rate of interest*. If velocity, however, turns out to be unpredictably variable, as it has indeed been in much of the postwar period, then demand does not totally create its own supply in the real world. In that case the supply response to an increase in demand has been *partial*. Kaldor allows for partial accommodation only toward the very end of his essay:

> When the response of the money supply is not complete—in other words when the money stock does not rise fully in proportion to the rise in expenditures—the velocity of circulation rises *to make up the difference*; in the opposite case it slows down. In other words, *changes in the stock of money and changes in velocity are substitutes to one another*. (Ibid., italics supplied)

Having said that, Kaldor does not retract his statement on the horizontal nature of the supply curve of money, nor is there any reason for him to do so. His initial diagram, apparently, stands unaltered. The reason is simple. For Kaldor, any shortfall in the increase in the supply of money will be met in full by a rise in velocity to "make up the difference," i.e., the *adjusted* or *effective* supply of money curve would be perfectly elastic and hence horizontal to the money axis. This follows inexorably from his statement that "changes in the stock of money and changes in velocity are substitutes to one another"—the implication being that they are *perfect* substitutes. If, however, money and the income velocity of money are less than perfect substitutes, if, in other words, the velocity increase does not fully "make up the difference," then the endogeneity of money does not imply a perfectly elastic or horizontal supply curve of money, and the relation of velocity to the rate of interest becomes an important consideration to be taken explicitly into account in any reformulation of an endogenous theory of the money supply, i.e., the rate of interest is no longer exogenously determined by the central bank and severed from the income velocity of money, as it is in Kaldor's theory of endogeneity via the lender of last resort argument.

The postwar behavior of the income velocity of money

Table 5.1 summarizes the postwar movements of the income velocity of money (defined as the ratio of nominal GNP to the Keynesian measure of the money supply as a means of payment, i.e., M1) from the Treasury-Federal Reserve Accord of March 1951 to the end of 1984. Also given, for each year, is the 3-month Treasury Bill rate for new issues as a proxy for the short-term interest rate. Table 5.1 also indicates the NBER cyclical turning points and the timing of Paul Volcker's monetarist policy shift of October 1979. The data of Table 5.1 are plotted in Figures 5.3 and 5.4.

It becomes immediately apparent that the Radcliffe Committee was correct in stating that it could find no "reason for supposing, or any experience in monetary history indicating, that there is any limit to the velocity of circulation." Whether it is a perfect substitute for increases in the conventional money supply, however, is another matter. At the inception of modern monetary policy in 1951, the velocity of circulation stood at 2.774. By 1981 it peaked at 6.892, or an increase of 148 percent, more than doubling in the process. The only significant drop in velocity comes in 1983 when it fell to 6.517—largely as a result of the massive deflation of the economy under the aegis of Volcker's monetarist policies, when the TB rate soared to an unprecedented 15.1 percent in 1981-III and the prime rate stood at over 20 percent. Figure 5.4 shows an upward sloping $V(i)$ curve for each expansion, with the curve taking a vertical posture for the recessions of 1969–70 and 1973–75. It is only in the major downturn of 1980–82 that velocity shows a tendency to decline. The right-hand part of Figure 5.4 dramatically indicates the consequences of the 1980s monetarist experiment. But even then the persistent rightward march of velocity was temporarily and moderately reversed in 1982 and 1983. By 1984 its forward movement was resumed.

The movement of velocity clearly reflects the financial sector's offsetting responses to the policies of the monetary authorities. The dramatic increases in velocity date from 1955, the first expansion after the Treasury-Federal Reserve Accord of March 1951 in which open market operations were aggressively used in a systematic way. The use of open market operations, in the United States, as the key discretionary policy tool was based on the assumption that they could be used to achieve an appropriate pattern of interest rates. The end

Table 5.1

The income velocity of money
(1951–1984)

Year		Real GNP	Nominal GNP	M1	V	i
1951	[A]	579.3	330.7	119.2	2.774	1.09
1952		600.8	348.0	125.2	2.780	1.77
1953	(P)	623.5	366.8	128.3	2.859	2.27
1954	(T)	611.8	363.8	129.7	2.805	0.92
1955		657.5	400.1	134.5	2.975	1.75
1956		671.5	421.7	136.0	3.101	2.66
1957	(P)	683.8	444.0	136.8	3.246	3.26
1958	(T)	681.0	449.6	138.4	3.249	1.83
1959		721.7	487.9	141.4	3.450	3.41
1960	(P)	732.1	504.8	142.0	3.555	2.36
1961	(T)	756.5	524.6	144.3	3.635	2.38
1962		800.3	565.0	147.9	3.820	2.78
1963		832.5	596.7	152.4	3.915	3.16
1964		876.4	637.7	158.3	4.028	3.55
1965		929.3	691.0	165.1	4.185	4.19
1966		984.8	756.0	172.6	4.380	4.97
1967		1,011.4	799.6	179.5	4.455	4.33
1968		1,058.1	873.4	192.1	4.547	5.35
1969	(P)	1,087.7	944.0	203.5	4.639	6.69
1970	(T)	1,086.4	992.7	211.2	4.700	6.44
1971		1,122.4	1,077.7	225.5	4.779	4.34
1972		1,185.9	1,185.9	241.7	4.906	4.07
1973	(P)	1,254.3	1,326.4	259.3	5.115	7.03
1974		1,246.3	1,434.2	272.2	5.269	7.88
1975	(T)	1,231.7	1,549.2	284.9	5.438	5.82
1976		1,298.2	1,718.0	301.1	5.706	5.00
1977		1,369.7	1,918.0	323.9	5.922	5.27
1978		1,438.6	2,156.1	350.6	6.150	7.22
1979	[V]	1,479.4	2,413.9	377.7	6.391	10.04
1980	(PT)	1,474.0	2,626.1	401.4	6.542	11.74
1981	(P)	1,502.6	2,954.1	428.6	6.892	14.08
1982	(T)	1,481.6	3,073.0	458.0	6.710	10.73
1983		1,534.8	3,309.4	507.8	6.517	8.62
1984		1,639.9	3,664.2	558.7	6.558	9.58

Key: [A] = Treasury-Federal Reserve Accord of March 1951, (P) = NBER cyclical peak, (T) = NBER cyclical trough, [V] = Volcker policy shift of October 1979, Real GNP in constant 1972 dollars, M1 = Currency, demand deposits and other checkable deposits, V = Nominal GNP/M1, i = 3-month Treasury Bill rate on new issues.
Sources: Department of Commerce National Income and Product Accounts, Economic Reports of the President, and Federal Reserve Bulletins, various years.

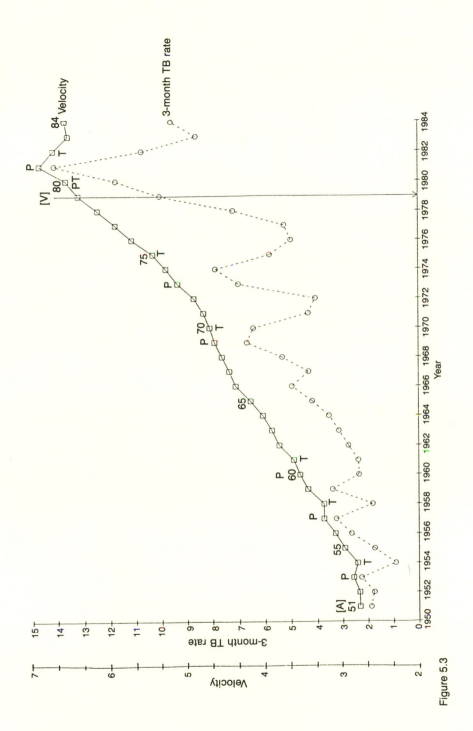

Figure 5.3

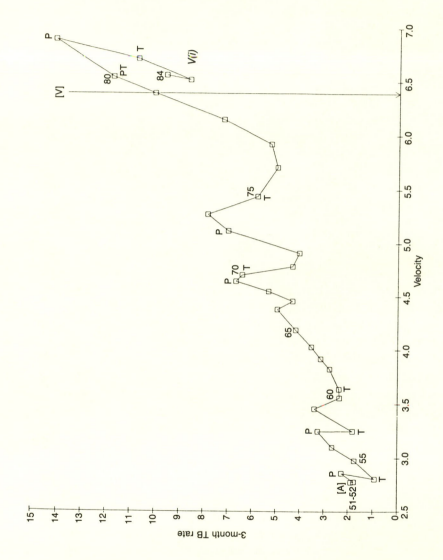

Figure 5.4

result was to trigger offsetting increases in the income velocity of money.

The Keynesian explanation of changes in velocity is covered in Chapter 3 in terms of the activation of idle balances and the economizing of transactions balances in response to central bank-induced increases in the rate of interest. This particular explanation entails a movement *along* a stable $V(i)$ curve as shown in Figure 3.3). The underlying assumption is that institutional relations and the financial structure of the economy have not changed. What remains to be done is to explain the *shifts* in the $V(i)$ curve which come about in response to the tight money policies of the central bank. The foremost explanation of the shifting theoretical $V(i)$ curves (which cut across the statistical $V(i)$ curve of Figure 5.4) is to be found in the rapid acceleration of financial innovations. The institutional structure of the financial sector of the economy has been in such turmoil, recently, that the very definition of money, let alone its measurement, has become problematical.

An alternative theory of the endogenous money supply

In a speech remarkable for its candor, Anthony M. Solomon, then President of the Federal Reserve Bank of New York, announced at a luncheon meeting of the American Economic and Financial Associations (December 28, 1981) that the country was "in the midst of a wave of innovation in the financial industry that amounts to a veritable revolution."[14] He referred to October 1979 when "a substantial change in [the Federal Reserve's] operating procedures was made with the primary objective of enhancing the achievement of our monetary targets" and emphasized that the new approach depended on the central bank's ability to devise a *measure* of the money supply that bore "a reasonably stable and predictable relation to broad economic conditions"—which is another way of stating that the money supply (whatever it may be) is exogenous and capable of being determined by the central bank, or, alternatively, that a stable link exists between M and Y. The "wave of financial innovation," however, was serving to undermine the link (assuming it ever existed except *in extremis*) in such a way that "even the very viability of the money stock targets is at stake." The central bank, in other words, was losing control because of new liquidity-providing instruments such as corporate overnight repurchase agreements (RPs), money market mutual funds, "sweep" accounts, new money market CDs, the burgeoning Eurodollar market, and so on—many of them capable of being used as transaction accounts virtually free of any meaningful reserve requirements. To compound the problem, the *Depository Institutions Deregulation and Monetary Control Act of 1980* was in the process of opening the floodgates to further innovations, with brokerage houses entering the banking business and thrift institutions allowed to operate in areas previously restricted to commercial banks. Conventional monetary policy has been seriously eroded by the explosion of financial innovations. The $V(i)$ curve, like the much-touted Phillips curve, is beginning to take on the attributes of a flying saucer. Lamented Mr. Solomon, "The world that will come into existence after the current wave of innovation and deregulation has spent its force is still, in many respects, unknown."

Hyman Minsky was among the first to focus on the issue of financial innovations and the problem they posed for monetary policy.[15] He was ignored. But even he, writing in 1957, could not have imagined the scope of what was yet to come. The essentials were in place and they turned out to be prophetic. Given an excess demand for money, Minsky argued, any attempt by the central bank to offset it would require a higher level of interest rates. The higher interest rates, however, would "induce institutional changes in the money market which [would] have the effect of increasing lending ability." Where a stable financial structure implies movement along a given $V(i)$ curve as an offset to monetary policy, financial innovations imply a shift of the curve in response to higher interest rates. In times of pronounced tight money, those institutional innovations will occur "which tend to increase velocity"—or, if the money supply is so severely constrained as to break the back of the economy (as it did in the early 1980s), the increase in velocity can be temporarily halted or even reversed, but at an excessive price in unemployment.

To recapitulate, the total increase in velocity in response to higher interest-rate levels corresponds to the sum of two effects: (1) movement along a given $V(i)$ curve before financial innovations have taken hold (i.e., by the activation of idle balances and the economizing of transactions balances), and (2) a shift of the $V(i)$ curve as a result of the innovations induced, during a prolonged expansion, by the higher interest-rate levels. In the first case, it is the opportunity cost of holding money at high interest-rate levels that causes a general activation of idle balances and the economizing of transactions balances by the business sector. The effect is largely on the demand side. In the latter case of financial innovations, the effect of high interest rates manifests itself principally on the supply side in response to credit rationing and the general unavailability of funds from conventional sources, which are reflected in the higher level of interest rates. The theory of an endogenous money supply must therefore incorporate velocity changes as a part of its explanation.

If the increase in the money supply does not fully accommodate the increase in the demand for money but velocity increases to make up the shortfall, then the horizontal money supply curve in the Kaldor diagram represents what can be called the *effective* money supply, not the conventional or direct money supply. The direct, or conventional, money supply is perfectly elastic *only* when the central bank increases the money supply to the full extent of the increase in the demand for money, in which case the income velocity of money is unchanged. But as the historical data indicate, velocity has not been constant—it has moved with the level of interest rates as shown in Figure 5.3 and 5.4. Whether the magnitude of the velocity changes is sufficient to produce a horizontal *effective* money supply is another matter. As Minsky put it, "These institutional changes [in addition to prior movements along a $V(i)$ curve, it should be added] may or may not lead to a sufficient increase in financing ability to affect the same increase in financing as would have occurred if there had been no central bank constraint" (p. 171). In other words, although velocity changes may accommodate an increase in the demand for money (by increasing the lending ability of a wide range of financial institutions), they do not necessarily result in a *full* accommodation. Indeed, the chances are they will not, Nicholas Kaldor to the contrary notwithstanding. It is highly doubtful that in the absence of full accommodation by the central bank velocity changes will rise "to make up the difference." At any rate, Kaldor gives no explanation of why this will always be the case. He merely assumes that velocity changes and increases in the conventional money supply are perfect substitutes.

The alternative restatement of the theory of an endogenous money supply can be made more explicit in terms of a diagram. In Figure 5.5 we start once again at the equilibrium point A where the demand and supply of money are equal at a given level of real output and employment determined by the interest rate i_8. As in the Weintraub model, an increase in unit labor costs shifts the demand for money curve from $D(Y)$ to $D(Y)'$. The demand for money now exceeds supply by the amount AB at the interest rate level i_8. The curve SM represents the traditional exogenous money supply approach where the central bank's refusal to increase the money supply would drive up the interest rate to i_{20}. If, for any reason, velocity were not able to respond to the higher rate of interest, the level of real output would fall by the amount needed to restore the initial equilibrium demand for money (albeit at a higher level of unemployment). Conversely, if the central bank were under orders to maintain the original output and employment levels, its "sustaining" operations would keep the interest rate at i_8 by allowing a full accommodation of the increased demand for money—leading to the S_M'

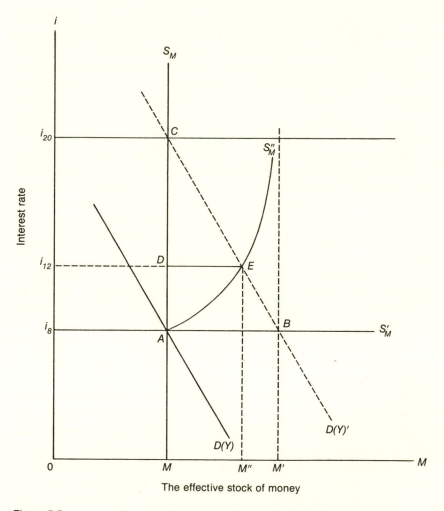

The effective stock of money

Figure 5.5

supply curve as a horizontal line, i.e., a fully endogenous direct money supply with velocity unchanged.

Alternatively, at no accommodation with the direct money supply held constant (assuming the central bank could in fact keep it so), velocity changes would take place at an accelerating pace as the interest rate moved upward from i_8 toward i_{20}. It is highly unlikely, however, that at any *feasible* interest rate the response of velocity would be sufficient to fill the excess demand gap of AB. In Figure 5.5, the *total*, or *effective*, supply curve of money (S_M'') is positively sloped reflecting the direct relationship of the total supply of money to the rate of interest. Where it intersects the $D(Y)'$ curve at i_{12}, nominal income at the higher price level will have fallen as a result of the fall in real output brought about by the higher rate of interest. In equilibrium at point E, demand is equal to total supply ($0M''$) with the latter being the sum total of the given direct ($0M$) and indirect ($MM'' = DE$) money supplies. Market forces will assure, *ceteris paribus*, the stability of the equilibrium at point E. Figure 5.5 could easily be adapted to represent the combination of a *partial* accommodation of the direct money supply, by a central bank wishing to avoid a severe debt deflation, and a smaller increase in velocity—with the sum total (at a lower interest rate) larger than $0M''$ but smaller than $0M'$ with an S_M'' curve intersecting the $D(Y)'$ curve somewhere between B and E. In either event, the supply curve of money is neither vertical, as traditional monetary theory would have it, nor perfectly elastic according to the more extreme Post Keynesian versions of the endogeneity of the money supply. It has the virtue, furthermore, of representing the state of "general liquidity" in the economy with its emphasis on the flow of credit as opposed to a more restrictive notion of the stock of money. Yet even in this modified and more realistic version, the traditional causal arrow is reversed with the supply of money (or, more accurately, credit) being demand-determined although not completely so—demand does not fully create its own supply; it does so only partially.

Even with this alternative explanation of the endogeneity of the money supply, a critical problem remains. With velocity changes (i.e., financial innovations) entering into the picture as offsets to conventional monetary policy, the effectiveness of monetary policy for controlling inflationary pressures in excess demand situations becomes seriously compromised.[16] Nevertheless, monetary policy can and does have an impact on the growth rate of the economy. Money does matter.

Moreover, given the pace of financial innovations in response to tight money conditions, the use of monetary policy to counteract the velocity changes involved would have to be so severe as to induce a major downturn in the economy, as in 1981–82. In the absence of Post Keynesian fine-tuning (an effective incomes policy plus a full-employment fiscal policy), monetary policy becomes a critical factor in the instability of the capitalist system. It cannot be wished away by saying that, if the money supply curve is not horizontal, it "ought" to be. Again, money matters. Changes in the income velocity of money due largely to financial innovations imply a loss of control over the flow of *credit* in the economy. Conventional monetary policy as practiced since 1955 has proved to be a failure on all counts—Keynesian as well as monetarist. An effective monetary policy must be able to deal with destabilizing developments in the financial sector of the economy. The traditional tools of open market operations, the discount rate, and manipulation of reserve requirements are no longer adequate. Keynes's concern in the *Tract* with the destabilizing effects of velocity changes have to be reconsidered, and doing so will require the redesigning of our monetary tools so as to allow some form of selective control over the flow of *credit* in the economy as a key part of any stabilization policy. But whether even this will be enough to solve capitalism's fundamental problem concerning the allocation and distribution of its surplus is highly questionable, especially within the restricted and essentially liberal-conservative approach of the American branch of Post Keynesian economics.

One final note needs to be added. Both Sidney Weintraub and Nicholas Kaldor developed their theories of the endogeneity of money as a counterpoint to the monetarist theories of Milton Friedman. But in so framing their arguments, they apparently missed an opportunity to question Keynes's liquidity preference theory and its formulation in terms of a money-bond model. The endogeneity model can be linked to a reinterpretation of Keynes's finance motive to emphasize that the demand for money is for financial credit primarily by the business sector and not for assets by the general public as in the *General Theory's* retrogression to a liquidity preference model. Linking the demand for money to the financing of investment and the problem of capital accumulation yields a far more promising prospect than the more limited use of the endogeneity thesis as a club with which to beat Milton Friedman over the head—as well as neoclassical Keynesians.

Notes

1. The model to be presented is based on Chapter 1, pages 28–30 of Sidney Weintraub's *Keynes, Keynesians, and Monetarists* (Philadelphia: University of Pennsylvania Press, 1978). His arguments on "endogeneity" are scattered throughout the book, but special attention should be given to Chapter 7, and particularly to Chapter 8, which was written with the collaboration of Paul Davidson. These chapters, however, are wide-ranging and do not tackle the subject matter at length or with detailed analysis. It is only in the few pages of Chapter 1 that a sustained analysis, however brief, can be found. At any rate, the variability of velocity as part of the explanation of endogeneity is not addressed and it is for that reason that the assumption of a constant velocity of money is introduced as an integral part of the Weintraub model. Justification for doing so is based on equation (6) of page 29 where ΔV *and* ΔQ are explicitly set at zero. Weintraub, of course, was well aware that V was anything but stable, but he did not incorporate this fact into his theory of endogeneity. The model that follows is faithful to Weintraub's view of the matter although it, and a later exposition via the use of Kaldor's diagram, is a reconstruction of his initial position not to be found as such in his writings. It will be used as a key paradigm of the Post Keynesian theory of an endogenous money supply.

2. For a discussion of the confusion surrounding this concept, see Peter J. Reynolds, "Kalecki's Degree of Monopoly," *Journal of Post Keynesian Economics*, Spring 1983. In Reynolds' interpretation, the degree of markup is exogenous to the theory of prices and distribution.

3. Weintraub, *Keynes*, p. 157, italics supplied.

4. This political theory of the endogeneity of money is an important critique of virtually all the econometric demand functions which have been estimated in the last three decades and helps one to understand why the monetarists have been so misguided.

5. Like Sidney Weintraub, Jan A. Kregel also argues the liberal position that monetary policy would never be used to cause large-scale unemployment. See J. A. Kregel, "From Post-Keynes to Pre-Keynes," *Social Research*, Summer 1979.

6. See note 3, Chapter 4, for citations of Basil Moore and Marc Lavoie. See also Hyman P. Minsky, *Can "It" Happen Again?* and Paul Davidson, "Why Money Matters," *Journal of Post Keynesian Economics*, Fall 1978, and *Money and the Real World*. See also the discussion of the finance motive in Chapter 3 above for the implicit assumption by the Davidson model of full accommodation.

7. Kaldor, *The Scourge of Monetarism* (London: Oxford University Press, 1982), p. 47, original italics.

8. Sidney Weintraub acknowledged Kaldor's priority but went on to wed his own wage theorem to Kaldor's aperçu. Kaldor's principal works on the endogenous money supply, apart from his latest formulation of it in the *Scourge* are: "The New Monetarism," *Lloyds Bank Review*, July 1970, and *The Origins of Monetarism* (1980). As early as 1959 Kaldor was arguing that the "spectacular rise in the velocity of circulation . . . fully compensated for the failure of the money supply to expand *pari passu* with the rise in prices and in money incomes . . . [I]f the supply of money had not been restricted, the increase in the velocity of circulation would not have taken place and it is a matter of doubt, to say the least, whether the course of prices and incomes would have been any different" (*Principal Memoranda of Evidence*, Vol. 3, Part XIII, p. 146, Radcliffe Committee). See also, F. W. Paish, "Business Cycles in Britain," *Lloyds Bank Review*, October 1970, pp. 11–12.

9. *The Origins of Monetarism*, quotations taken from pp. 8, 9, and 15, original italics.

10. *Scourge*, p. 24, italics supplied.

11. That this formulation is widely accepted by American Post Keynesian monetary economists is more than amply illustrated in the introduction to a forthcoming collection of essays on the endogeneity of the money supply (to be published by M. E. Sharpe, Inc.). The editor, Alfred Eichner, argues in his "Introduction" as follows for the pre-October 1979 period: "[T]he supply curve is perfectly elastic, and thus runs parallel to the horizontal axis at a height equal to the prevailing interest rate . . . [T]he Fed's overriding objective was to protect the liquidity position of the commercial banks. The *fully* accommodating behavior which this strategy dictated led to a supply curve for both bank deposits and currency which . . . was perfectly elastic" (italics supplied). Eichner's "Introduction" represents a summary of the Post Keynesian consensus on the issue of endogeneity. It is strictly Kaldorian.

12. Sidney Weintraub, *Capitalism's Inflation and Unemployment Crisis* (Reading, Mass.: Addison-Wesley, 1978), p. 193.

13. Kaldor, *Scourge*, p. 29, original italics.

14. Anthony M. Solomon, "Financial Innovation and Monetary Policy," December 28, 1981; reprinted by the Federal Reserve Bank of New York, 1982.

15. Hyman Minsky, "Central Banking and Money Market Changes," *Quarterly Journal of Economics*, May 1957; reprinted in *Can "It" Happen Again?* (Armonk, N. Y.: M. E. Sharpe, Inc., 1982).

16. Any attempt by the central bank to offset velocity changes by a further restriction of the money supply would only serve to cause a further increase in velocity through a second round of financial innovations, and so on. It was this continuous slippage that became the primary concern of the Radcliffe Committee although, in the end, the committee had a monumental failure of nerve.

CHAPTER 6

The policy implications of Post Keynesian monetary theory

The unity of theory and praxis

Any theory in reasonable contact with reality carries with it a plan for action—a policy for changing the world along better lines in keeping with its vision. When a theory is devoid of any contact with reality, it has no policy implications (action in the real world not being possible), or, alternatively, if a theory has but a tenuous contact with reality, its policy implications may be irrelevant or politically impractical. Neo-classical Keynesian theory, by virtue of its reformulation of Keynes along general equilibrium lines, has been moving along the latter trajectory. Post Keynesian theory, on the other hand, represents an attempt, still in the process of being worked out, to restore reality to economic thinking in terms of the power relationships of contemporary society. Whether it has done so effectively, or any better than neoclassical Keynesianism along politically practical lines, is left to the concluding section of this chapter.

The Radcliffe Committee's general liquidity thesis raised the issue of the endogeneity of the "money supply" obliquely. It did not identify it as such, but it did stress the *elasticity of the credit structure* and the shifts in the $V(i)$ curve via financial innovations that reduced the open market operations of pre-monetarist monetary policy (in the United States) to a state of ineffectiveness. The committee's emphasis was on the issue of general liquidity and the flow of *credit* in the economy, particularly to the "Industrial" sector that Keynes emphasized in his *Treatise*. Investment had a financial dimension that could not be ignored in a credit-money economy. The liquidity preference theory of

Keynes's later *General Theory* should have been dropped in favor of a theory stated in terms of the demand for credit, not assets. Here, the finance motive of 1937 could have been better formulated.

The issue of controlling the flow of credit through the economy and coming to terms with the offsetting effects of a rapid rate of financial innovation remains with us to this day—even more so than it did in Keynes's time or that of the Radcliffe Committee. An early attempt to restore some measure of reality to the realm of monetary policy can be found in Volume 3, part XIII, of the Radcliffe Committee's *Memoranda of Evidence*.

The British economists who gave testimony had most of the basic elements of contemporary Post Keynesian economics in place. They rejected the idea that a predominant emphasis on monetary policy could achieve stability at full employment, and they prophetically anticipated the consequences of the "monetarist" policies of the Thatcher and Reagan administrations of the early 1980s. The long-run expectations of the monetarists were bound to be falsified by the short-run consequences of their policies. The long run is not impervious to the short-run shocks that monetarist policies would themselves induce. At best, monetary policy could only support fiscal policy in a subordinate capacity. Yet key contributors to the *Memoranda*, in 1959, even rejected the notion that an optimum combination of monetary and fiscal policy existed. Not even Samuelson's artificial restoration of Say's law through the "skillful use of fiscal and monetary policy" could succeed in forcing the economy "into behaving like a neoclassical model."

The strongest argument came from A. J. Brown of the University of Leeds. Given that prices are a markup over prime costs and the degree of monopoly in the economy is relatively stable, then profit variations are due primarily to variations in the level of economic activity (capacity utilization). Insofar as traditional monetary policy has little, if any, direct effect on prime costs, its principal effect will not be on prices but on the level of output and hence on profits. If carried to an extreme, monetary policy can, of course, lower the rate of inflation, but only by raising the unemployment rate to record levels. In the words of Brown, "In an industrial economy the compression of profit margins does not seem to be a very promising field for attack upon price inflation by monetary policy. The immediate effect is likely to reduce production (probably with increased total cost per unit) rather than price reduction."[1] For Brown, the cost of labor is the main determinant of prices, and since monetary policy has little influence over wage and salary negotiations, it is unlikely to have any direct influence on prices. Its effect can only be *indirect*—when monetary policy is carried to such an extreme as to cause massive unemployment, with trade union power seriously compromised as a result. The real costs of an "effective" monetary policy are therefore to be found in the serious under employment of labor and equipment and in the slowing down of the rate of technological innovation.

R. F. Kahn was equally forceful in stating the case:

> It is the rise in wages which is the cause of prices rising . . . The normal situation is . . . one in which the behaviour of prices is determined by the course of wage negotiations, so that any progressive rise in prices is a "cost inflation" . . . If reliance is placed on regulation of demand in order to secure a tolerable behaviour of prices, it must certainly mean maintaining unemployment at a level which would represent very serious economic waste . . . The economic waste involved in such a policy is particularly great if demand is regulated by restricting productive investment, *as will be the main result of relying on monetary policy.* (P. 142, italics supplied)

The solution to the problem of maintaining a stable price level is not to be found in monetary policy, but "in the realm of wage negotiations." In short, an *incomes policy* is a prerequisite for price stability. To attempt to achieve it through monetary policy would end in perverse results. Nicholas Kaldor, for example, flatly denied any direct relationship between the money supply and the level of nominal income. "To proceed from one to the other," he argued in 1959, "it is necessary to postulate that changes in the supply of money leave the frequency with which money changes hands (the so-called 'velocity of circulation') unaffected" (p. 146). A change in the money supply, in Kaldor's opinion, had no "impact effect . . . on the level of payments" (p. 146). The only effect was on the velocity of circulation. Kaldor went on to agree with Brown and Kahn that monetary policy is effective only *in extremis*, i.e., by such "drastic steps in raising interest rates" that unemployment would increase to unprecedented postwar levels (as indeed it did under the high interest rates of the early 1980s) and the functioning of the capital and credit markets would be destabilized (as they in fact were). The speculative motive would swamp the enterprise motive, in Keynes's terms, "and long-run considerations of relative profitability would play a subordinate role in the allocation of funds" (p. 148). In the end, Kaldor agreed with Brown and Kahn.

> [W]hen the driving force behind inflation is an excessive rate of increase in money wages . . . [the problem of controlling] wage inflation . . . is not one that can be expected to be cured by restrictions of demand—not unless the restriction is carried to the point of such heavy unemployment that the wage earners in any particular industry are unable to hold out for higher wages.

The failure of nerve

The Radcliffe Committee Report ignored the testimony of the British economists and put all of its hopes on the central bank's ability to affect the term structure of interest rates.

> [A] movement of rates of interest, quite apart from any direct effect it may have on the demand for investment [which the committee thought was little enough] may have appreciable [*sic*] effects on the behaviour of various financial institutions . . . *Provided that it is not confined to the short end of the market*, a movement of interest rates implies significant changes in the capital values of many assets held by financial institutions.[2]

The balance sheet, or wealth effects, of interest rate policy was brought into full play as a counterbalance to the committee's dismissal of the interest incentive effect, on the demand side, as a cost to borrowers. For the committee, this was "an important conclusion for policy" since it implied "that movements in interest rates have an effect apart from any influence they have on the incentive to hold capital goods" (p. 134)—the latter being, of course, minimal within the prevailing range of interest-rate variation existing at that time.

The Radcliffe Committee had shifted to the supply side with its emphasis on playing the full maturity spectrum of government securities. Given the "locking-in effect," which is nowhere referred to as such in the *Report*, it is the "*structure* of interest rates rather than some notion of the 'supply of money' . . . [which becomes] *the centre-piece of monetary action*" (p. 18, italics supplied). The "locking-in-effect" argued that the large postwar debt held by financial institutions made them susceptible to significant capital losses by relatively small changes (actual or threatened) in the relevant interest rates by the monetary authorities. Unwilling to face such losses, conservative financial institutions would not be willing to liquidate debentures in order to finance an increased demand for loans (credit). Interest rates, as in "bastard" Keynesian theory, were to be the key to a proper use of monetary policy, but not via the IS-LM analysis of the neoclassical synthesis. It would now be predominantly the supply-side effects of interest-rate changes *over the full maturity spectrum* of government securities that would do the trick.

In reflecting on its own general liquidity thesis, however, the committee became uncomfortable with what it had wrought and readily acknowledged the negative implications of its own novel approach to monetary policy:

> [I]f we are right in believing that the level of total demand is influenced by the lending behaviour of an *infinitely wide range of financial institutions*, and not just the supply of money, it might be supposed that we should substitute for the traditional control of the money supply a complex of controls over that wide range of financial institutions. Such a prospect would be unwelcome *except as a last resort*, not mainly because of its administrative burdens, but because *the further growth of new financial institutions would allow the situation continually to slip from the grip of the authorities*. (P. 134, italics supplied)

The committee then went on to reassure itself:

> The fact that operations on the structure of interest rates do, for institutional reasons, change the liquidity of financial operators *throughout the economy* should make it possible to avoid any such complex of direct controls. (P. 134, italics supplied)

Reliance on non-monetary measures and resort to "a comprehensive structure of financial controls" became admissible only in desperate straights. The argument of the committee that controls would cause "the further growth of . . . financial institutions," thus allowing "the situation continually to slip from the grip of the authorities," is no more than a reflection of their earlier statement that they could not find "any reason for supposing . . . that there is any limit to the velocity of circulation of money." Given this continuous slippage, which would only be accelerated by resort to comprehensive controls, they sought desperate refuge in the efficacy of the locking-in effect. But if the locking-in effect does not work, which it doesn't, because of the very low average maturity of the public debt and if financial innovations are rampant, then, on the Radcliffe Committee's own terms, there is no other recourse than to "a complex [system] of controls"—the very thing the committee wished to avoid "except as a last resort." The committee had a clear failure of nerve. Although the door was wide open for selective controls over a wide range of financial institutions, the Radcliffe Committee slammed the door shut on the implications of its own general liquidity thesis. It failed to face up to the issue, emphasized in its *Report*, of a runaway income velocity of money and the need to address that issue in terms of direct monetary controls.

It is interesting to note, at this point, that Keynes, in his *Tract on Monetary Reform* (1923), was at that time a very uncomfortable quantity theorist. Although accepting the quantity theory's causal arrow from the quantity of money to the general price level, he refused to accept the implied stability of the velocity of circulation. Keynes went so far as to argue that changes in *M* and changes in *V* were *interrelated* through changes in the amount of reserves that banks would hold against their deposit liabilities. The equi-proportionality requirement of the standard quantity theory of money would therefore not hold. Keynes also raised the possibility that "habits and practices, once changed, will not revert to exactly their old shape." In that event the exact proportionality requirement would not hold even in the very long run, leaving important doubts concerning the overall effectiveness of monetary policy. To counteract shifts in the mood of the public and the business world, Keynes thought that the bank rate could be used to counteract the troubling changes in *V* (or *k*, in the Cambridge version) in order to achieve stability in the price level. Keynes, of course, was placing his bets on the effectiveness of the interest-incentive effect on borrowers, i.e., on the demand side.[3] It was not until the *Treatise* and finally in the *General Theory* that Keynes cracked the classical dichotomy, downgrading monetary policy in the process, whereas the Radcliffe Committee in 1959 was trying desperately to resurrect monetary policy in a new and more effective form.

Direct monetary controls

On the issue of direct controls, the *Memoranda of Evidence* gets quickly to the point. A few choice quotations will serve the purpose:

> [T]he problem [is] . . . whether central bank policy can . . . be made more effective . . . without varying the rate of interest, through direct

controls of the volume of bank credit and forcing, in the ultimate analysis, credit rationing on the banks without moral suasion and appeals. (P. 35)

—Thomas Balogh

[M]onetary controls provide a very unreliable and clumsy method of regulating investment. Some differentiation of rates should be possible as between one industry and another and one type of investment and another. (P. 146)

—R. F. Kahn

[I]t is unlikely that changes in interest rates can themselves be relied on to have much effect . . . Changes in the supply of funds available for borrowing (i.e., credit restriction . . . or direct rationing of credit) may have rather more effect. (P. 163)

—I. M. D. Little et al.

The power of direct controls in England existed long before the Radcliffe Committee undertook its investigation on the working of the monetary system. Under Clause 4 of the Act of 1946, as R. S. Sayers pointed out, "The Bank of England can issue directions compelling bankers, for example, to hold certain reserves with itself . . . *It may [also] compel bankers to favour one industry or group of industries as borrowers.*"[4] Sayers was one of the key members of the Radcliffe Committee. The sixth edition of his book, *Modern Banking*, is of special interest since it incorporated some of the major findings of the Radcliffe Committee. Sayers, however, did not pick up on the issue of selective credit controls, limiting himself instead to what can best be called "moral suasion with a stick"—or the *threat* of selective controls to induce compliance. It is not a very convincing argument, and certainly not one to be applied to the U.S. monetary system with its 14,000 banks compared to Britain's handful, but at least by 1964 Sayers had retreated from the locking-in effect argument of the Radcliffe Committee.[5] Nevertheless, Sayers did recognize that the "choice is between an emphasis on raising interest rates and on direct interference with banks and other financial intermediaries by raising liquidity ratio requirements [a combination of cash and very short term liquid earning assets] and/or *direct restraints on lending.*" Since the "interest-incentive effect is slow to operate," the choice for Sayers was "*between administrative cumbersomeness on the one hand and inequity and inefficiency on the other*" (p. 257, italics supplied).

The need for selective monetary controls stems directly from the ineffectiveness of traditional monetary policy—its "inequity and inefficiency''—particularly as a result of *shifts* in the *V*(*i*) curve due to financial innovations. The last ten years have witnessed a veritable revolution in the financial structure of the American economy. It has made a shambles of open market operations. The attempt to control the money supply by putting pressure on bank reserves has been put to rout by the development of CDs and the Eurodollar market in the 1960s, and more recently by sweep accounts, money market funds, NOW accounts, Super NOW accounts, the entry of brokerage houses and credit card companies into the banking business, and on and on. And with the Monetary Control Act of 1980 close to full implementation, the future will bring with it an even more radically changed financial structure. The very concept of the "money supply" has already become virtually meaningless and the attempt to control something that cannot be accurately defined, let alone measured, is itself a measure of the madness afoot.

It is the *elasticity of the credit structure* that has become and will continue to be *the* problem, much of it in response to the monetarist targeting of all-elusive monetary aggregates, with money market interest rates set free to find their unhindered market levels. Monetary policy has become an exercise in futility. *Nous pedalons dans la choucroute*, as French wit would put it. In Radcliffe terms, the "liquidity structure" has been transformed by the radically changing complex of financial claims to such an extent that there no longer is any direct relationship between it and the long-term growth of the economy, with banks now "playing a relatively smaller part than before." In the words of R. S. Sayers:

> There is no fixed barrier between what is and what is not banking, and how important banks are, and how important are other financial intermediaries, depends upon the extent to which innovation of financial devices is shared by banks or is left to the ingenuity of financiers outside the banks. (P. 174)

The banks, however, are fighting back under the changes wrought by the Monetary Control Act of 1980, and the outcome of the fierce competition now taking place between banks and nonbank financial intermediaries cannot be predicted; but what can be predicted is an acceleration in the pace of financial innovations with the progressive fudging between what is and what is not a bank. In the process, the monetarists' much-touted stability of the demand for money function has taken off the way of the Phillips curve. It is clearly spinning out of control.

Government policy cannot ignore these developments. As in the theory of evolution, changes do not take place uniformly in time. Periods of relative stasis, as in the postwar period up to 1960, suddenly become periods of rapid change. Instead of gradual changes we are confronted with a profound temporal irregularity[6] which swamps our traditional control variables. Yet we persist in our addiction to general monetary controls because of our ideological bent for market solutions. Such limited policies are meant to affect the environment within which individual decisions are made without consciously singling out any particular individual—the impact on particular individuals depending on the state of their individual asset preferences, or the changes induced in such preferences by changes in the intensity of indirect controls. What is usually ignored is that the impact of a change in general controls (which are assumed to be more compatible with the values of a democratic society) will be unequal in its effect on different individuals, or groups of individuals, when differences in market power exist. As long as market power is unequally distributed, and asset preferences conditioned by that inequality exist, general controls will themselves be selective in their impact. The pattern of asset preferences is clearly not independent of the power constellations in the economy. And if the effects of general controls are not randomly distributed, they must of necessity follow the established channels of power, with the consequence that existing power differences are further reinforced and expanded. There is no such thing as a "neutral" monetary policy.

As currently constituted, monetary policy does not intervene by design into particular markets or sectors of the economy. The central bank does not have the power or the means to encourage expansion in depressed sectors or markets, or to restrain other sectors or markets where further expansion would result in economic disharmonies. If an excessive (speculative) rate of growth in one or more sectors of the economy introduces distortions which threaten the stability of the whole, indirect controls are faced with a dilemma. Either they permit the disequilibrating expansion to continue, or general restraints are introduced which, to a greater or lesser degree, affect other sectors of the economy as they flow selectively through the power channels of the economy. If some sectors low on the power scale were initially depressed, their situation worsens. If, on the other hand, they were expanding at a reasonable rate, they should have been encouraged or at least left alone. In either case the overall results are not conducive to general stability. And if these general, or "quantitative," monetary controls have only a minimal effect on the unduly expanding sectors because of their overriding speculative profit expectations, the net result is worse than if nothing at all had been done.

All this is true enough for a stable financial structure, but when the structure is in motion it, itself, becomes a significant part of the problem. Adherence to the traditional modes of monetary policy, whether of the Keynesian or monetarist variety, serves only to aggravate the inherent instability of the system. A more effective instrument of control would be *direct* or purposively selective financial controls over the full range of financial institutions. What we are faced with is what Sayers referred to as the choice "between administrative cumbersomeness on the one hand, and inequity and inefficiency on the other." The widespread antipathy toward selective controls is a prejudice steeped in a touching, if not convenient, belief in the ability of "free" markets to allocate financial and real resources with optimal efficiency. It never helps economic analysis to deal in terms of the untenable dualism of "freedom" versus "control." Indeed, control in many instances is a precondition for the realization of freedom in the larger sense. Moreover, many so-called "free" markets invariably promote and protect the "freedom" of the big and the powerful.

Selective control proposals

Keynes, himself, in the *Treatise*, was not opposed, as a matter of dogma, to the use of selective controls to influence the allocation of credit between the industrial and financial sectors of the economy or, for that matter, to cope with destabilizing developments in one of the sectors. Under certain conditions he favored discriminating "in terms of lending (either the rate charged or by rationing the amount) between the financial and industrial borrowers."[7]

The only place in the American literature, however, where one can find a systematic, albeit brief, discussion of selective controls is in E. A. Goldenweiser's neglected study of the development of American monetary policy from the founding of the Federal Reserve System in 1913 to 1950.[8] One long-standing proposal is for a *velocity reserve requirement* which would, after abolishing the distinction between demand and time deposits, determine the level of required reserves not only on the volume of all bank deposits but also on their rate of turnover. Another is the *dual reserve proposal*, which is, in effect, a ceiling reserve plan that diminishes the ability of banks to engage in the multiple expansion of deposits. After an announced date, all *new* deposits would be required to hold a larger proportion in reserves than for deposits in place before the announcement of the central bank. The plan is seen as an emergency measure to be applied in a rapidly developing inflationary situation. The reserve requirement on new deposits could be scaled up to 100 percent, which would, at that upper limit, prevent any use of these deposits for the issuance or renewal of loans. By design it would not in any way interfere with how and to whom banks allocate their available funds. Market considerations would, presumably, prevail, although credit rationing and personal discrimination would be more likely. Their only impact would be on the credit creation multiplier. Another advantage of the dual reserve proposal is that it would allow "the Federal Reserve to finance a large volume of credit for war or national security . . . in the least inflationary way" (p. 66) by exempting the purchase of government securities from the plan. Australia's use of the dual reserve plan was even more far reaching. *All* new deposits, after a certain date, had to be deposited with the central bank. In effect, they were impounded and then released on a selective basis for use in approved loans. The dual reserve proposal therefore did much more than just control the quantity of money; it also directed the flow of credit into desired channels—to specific sectors or industries of the economy.

To further strengthen the dual reserve proposal, use could be made of a complementary *supplementary reserve proposal* in which financial institutions would be required to hold a certain proportion of their reserves in the form of government securities, either in the form of general issues or special issues designed specifically for that purpose. The interest rate on such issues would be determined by the Treasury, not by the market, which would hold down the cost of servicing the public debt and amount to the payment of interest on a part of a bank's required reserve balances. As Goldenweiser points out, the supplementary reserve proposal is not a true reserve requirement since "the essence of reserves is that they are impounded or idle money, while requirements in the form of obligatory holdings of specified earning assets by member banks would not limit total earning assets of these banks . . . They would merely prevent conversion of public debt into private debt in member-bank portfolios" and provide "a means of immobilizing a certain portion of public debt and reducing the effect of tightening credit conditions on yields of government securities" (p. 61). The supplementary reserve proposal is, in a sense, a method of sterilizing government debt and removing it from the income distribution effects of the market's handling of the debt. Properly synchronized with the traditional open market operations of the central bank, it could also meet the much-touted problem of the "crowding-out effect" of Treasury financing.

All of these proposals, however, are designed for use in an over–full employment economy under inflationary strain. Their use, in reverse, in a deflationary situation, or in any fashion in the event of stagflation, raises the problem of "pushing on a string" or the need simultaneously to move in two opposite directions at one and the same time. A far more comprehensive proposal, which would not be subject to these problems, is the *asset reserve proposal*—by far the most important and, at the same time, least considered of all the proposals. It directly confronts the problem of velocity that so confounded Keynes in his *Tract on Monetary Reform*. The asset reserve proposal would shift the reserve requirement from the liability to the asset side of the balance sheet. Moreover, different reserve requirements could be applied to different classifications of assets, as well as a lower reserve requirement on government securities, in return for which a lower interest rate could be paid while giving government securities a preferential status.[9]

Under the asset reserve proposal, the monetary authorities would not be dealing directly with "money" but with the asset structure of commercial banks on the other side of the balance sheet. The loan part of bank earning-assets could easily be differentiated by industry or by sectors of the economy in keeping with the long-run development or growth plans of the government. The *flow of credit* through the economy would be controlled by green, amber, and red lights in the form of different asset reserve requirements. Financial institutions would still be free to make their own determinations as to where they wish to allocate their available reserves, subject of course to increasing penalties in the form of higher reserve requirements if they choose to go contrary to the overall guidelines and not comply "voluntarily" with the central bank's wishes.

The penalty aspects of the differentiated asset reserve proposal is an approach similar to the tax-based incomes policy (TIP) as applied to money wages. Banks would, of course, be free to set their own interest rates (just as firms under TIP would still be free to determine their own product prices) but they would be forced to impose considerably higher rates on those loans requiring higher reserve requirements, particularly in view of the fact that banks include required reserves as part of their internal cost of funds over which a markup is imposed to determine their lending rates. But this would only serve to reinforce the asset reserve proposal, while insulating the interest rate on the public debt from such pressures. The asset reserve proposal is obviously not a cure-all; it is simply a way of coping with the slippery changes in velocity. Open market operations, however, would not disappear. They would still be used, in a *supportive* way, to influence the level of deposits that the asset reserve proposal would then prod in the various directions desired.

In summary, if the central bank wanted to divert the *flow of credit*, say, into a depressed sector or industry or, for that matter, away from a sector in the throes of a speculative binge, it could adjust its reserve requirements accordingly to the point, in the latter case, of shutting off the flow entirely by hiking the reserve requirement to 100 percent. Alternatively, when warranted, if could as in the case of the Australian central bank direct banks to extend credit along particular lines at considerably lower, if not zero, reserve requirements, in compensation.

The important point is that the asset reserve proposal would adequately control the velocity of monetary circulation by not leaving it to the whims of bank decisions or the financial innovations induced by high interest rates—although it would have no direct control over changes in velocity due to a more intense corporate use of internal funds or their dumping of short-term governments and other highly liquid near-monies. At least a major, if not determining, factor in velocity changes will have been brought under control.

One final proposal, though extreme, does serve the purpose of focusing on an important issue. It is the *100 percent reserve proposal*. Under it the money supply would be completely controlled by the government and would be "regulated solely in the public interest, *without reference to risks and profits by which a money-market enterprise must necessarily be guided.*" It would not be subject or incidental to "actions of private organizations determined on the basis of considerations not related to the proper total volume of money."[10] Profit-making business enterprises, in other words, would be barred from creating money, as they do under a fractional reserve banking system, by the simple expedient of placing a 100 percent reserve requirement against all deposits. Control of the money supply would be squarely in the hands of the government, and credit would be allocated by the various regional central banks under guidelines set by the government in power. This is obviously the most controversial proposal of all. The original version was favored by economists at the University of Chicago (and a few others) before the takeover of that institution by Milton Friedman.

A more practical proposal, relatively speaking, would be to end the supposed "independence" of the central bank by putting it under the control of the Treasury Department.[11] When monetary policy was not as prominent as it is today, and when fiscal policy ruled the roost in the early postwar years, the "independence" of the Federal Reserve was of little importance. But with the marked shift toward a major emphasis on monetary policy, which began with the Accord of 1951 and then with the rise of monetarism in the 1960s, the issue of independence becomes critical. When responsibility "for" is minimal, responsibility "to" is irrelevant, but when responsibility "for" what is largely the elected government's responsibility increases, namely, the optimal functioning of the economy in line with the government's policy objectives, then responsibility "to" the elected officials is unavoidable—at least in a democracy which properly holds those elected officials responsible for whatever goes wrong. As it is, the "independence" of the Federal Reserve is largely a myth and, this being so, the pretense should be dropped.

Another alternative to the 100 percent reserve proposal (but not to the asset reserve proposal, which should be implemented) is the creation of a cabinet level Department of Economic Affairs, within which both the Treasury and the Federal Reserve would be subsumed. It would parallel, and for similar reasons, the establishment of the Department of Defense in the postwar period, which absorbed within it the Army, Navy, and Air Force departments. The secretary of each service lost cabinet rank in the reshuffling. The Secretary of Economic Affairs, like the Secretary of Defense, would alone hold cabinet rank and be responsible for the full coordination of economic policy. The security of a country depends as much, if not more, on the performance of the economy as it does on its national security defense preparations. And since defense expenditures are "cycle proof" and drain the resources of the economy more markedly in a protracted downturn than in a recovery, the Department of Economic Affairs, properly run, could lighten the relative burden of defense and better provide for the security of the nation. However organized, the asset reserve proposal should be one of its key objectives for coming to grips with the offsetting changes in velocity through a selective control over the flow of credit in the economy.

The instability of capitalism

One of the basic arguments of American Post Keynesians is that capitalism is an inherently unstable system which operates within a credit-money economy under conditions of uncertainty. They then go on to argue that it has successfully devised the means for coping with the related problems of instability and uncertainty by a rearrangement of its institutional structure. Two of the major proponents of this thesis are Paul Davidson and Hyman Minsky.[12] According to Davidson (and J. A. Kregel), given the volatility in the state of expectations in a world of uncertainty, and the operation of capitalism in historical time—where all forms of neoclassical equilibrium models are irrelevant and misleading—capitalism is of necessity unstable and would have collapsed a long time ago were it not for its ingenuity. By inventing *forward contracts* in money terms, business firms are able to put in place their own form of an incomes policy which, to a large extent, allows them to cope with uncertainty by contractually arranging for stable output and factor prices, i.e., for the sale of the goods they produce and for their wage and materials costs. These forward contracts, however, could easily break down in a crisis, leading to violent instability and the collapse they are supposed to forestall. A "catastrophic breach" of forward contracts cannot be allowed to happen. There must be a means of enforcing them, for they are "the most important economic institution yet devised for controlling the uncertain future course of markets." Their enforceability gives rise to a form of "wage and price controls" that allow capitalists to function in a world constantly threatened with catastrophe. The establishment of a relative stability of expectations in an uncertain world therefore requires the existence of contract-enforcing institutions, that is, the courts and the government. It is the state and its enforcement of the "rules of the game," so to speak, that guarantees the stability of the system by effectively counteracting its inherent tendency toward disaster.

This is a strange and very incomplete theory in that it almost totally suppresses history in its *political* context. When the private economic power of an economy and the state collaborate symbiotically to change the institutional framework for their mutual advantage, or to prevent changes needed to meet valid social discontents, social instability could be promoted leading to collapse, even if the courts dutifully enforced every clause of every single forward contract. Means of coping with and preventing *legitimation crises* through a more equitable distribution of the social product and a rising standard of living are better candidates for explaining the success and long stability of capitalism than the enforceability of forward contracts.

The same objections can be applied, *mutatis mutandis*, to Hyman Minsky's arguments. His theory of an ever-present potential collapse is based on an analysis of assets and a three-tiered structure of Hedge, Speculative, and Ponzi financing (see Chapter 2 above)—upon which the instability of capitalism is founded. He develops an endogenous theory of the business cycle based on shifts in his spectrum of financing toward the speculative and Ponzi ends that lead to financial instability and ultimate collapse in a major debt deflation, i.e., when the debt structure of the economy cannot be validated. However, all is not lost. "Once endogenous economic processes take the economy to the brink of crisis," he writes, "Federal Reserve intervention can abort the development of a full-fledged crisis and debt deflation" by promptly exercising its power of lender of last resort—thereby providing the necessary liquidity to prevent collapse. But this is only one half of the stabilization process, as Minsky sees it. The other half is big government and its discretionary and built-in, automatic, contracyclical fiscal policies. Government deficits "sustain income or increase corporate profits, and feed secure and negotiable financial instruments into portfolios hungry for safety and liquidity." Minsky's analysis reminds one, uncomfortably, of the artificial restoration of Say's law via the "skillful use of fiscal and monetary policy." It has some of the trappings of the neoclassical synthesis of "bastard" Keynesianism.

Of course, it is not just any kind of government intervention that counts. It has to be the right kind—the kind that fits, in a counteracting way, into Minsky's endogenous theory of the business cycle. After all, not all deficits are the same. It depends on the sources of revenue and the types of expenditures. The deficits of the Reagan administration do not fit the bill. *Their* purpose was to redistribute income in favor of capital which, if taken to extremes, could have destabilized the system in a way having nothing to do with the threat of a debt deflation. Minsky's "financial instability hypothesis" is a rather mechanical one and has the flavor of being designed *ex post* to explain what was, and what already is, as interpreted by his basic theory. There is the strange feeling that Minsky's theory is a combination of Samuelson's fine-tuning abilities and the central bank's ability to act as lender of last resort.

Yet, the vulnerability of capitalism is more than just a monetary phenomenon and both Davidson and Minsky, more so, are in danger of establishing a "neo-monetarism" based on a truncated version of Post Keynesian theory. Both, it would seem, are engaged in a convenient reductionism that is more understandable than it is acceptable. The threat to capitalism, in good Schumpeterian terms, is that of unexpected *exogenous* shocks to the system, not all of them economic in nature—but that is another story.[13]

For a greater part of the postwar period, fiscal policy was the primary tool for keeping the system on an even keel, and it failed. The more recent dominance of monetary over fiscal policy has failed even more miserably. It was the failure of neoclassical "Keynesianism without tears" and its fine-tuning nostrums that opened the door to the simplistic monetarist counterrevolution. The increasing reliance on monetary policy ("money matters") by neoclassical Keynesians and those who followed in their footsteps[14] succeeded in reducing the level of real output while failing to control inflation, giving birth to the "stagflation" neologism in the end.

The reason for this failure, according to Kaldor, was that "fiscal and monetary polic[ies] were brought to bear to ensure the full utilization of resources but they were unavailing for dealing with wage-induced inflation . . . [F]ull employment requires a *permanent incomes policy* . . . a policy of restraint on personal incomes . . . [and] the attainment of some consensus over the distribution of income between wages and profits."[15]

Even with a permanent incomes policy in place, full employment with a stable price level cannot be achieved without some regard for the financing of autonomous demand by loans in a credit-money economy. The monetary side must be brought into the analysis. But it must be done so in recognition that the "money supply" is *endogenous* (though not fully so) and that monetary control must therefore entail some measure of control over disequilibrating changes in the financial structure. Traditional monetary policy with its fixation on the money supply as an exogenous entity (whether based on neoclassical Keynesian or monetarist theory) is no longer tenable. Its postwar record warrants the conclusion.

Open market operations were discovered accidentally in 1923. They were not fully understood in the prewar period and even when used they were either inadequate or perversely applied. Modern monetary policy and the active use of open market operations dates from 1955, four years after the Treasury–Federal Reserve Accord. It has been around, in other words, for less than thirty years, and in that brief time it has been buffeted by a series of theories, from the availability of credit doctrine, to the bills-only policy, to the fine-tuning of neoclassical Keynesianism, to the rules of monetarism—none of which worked for the obvious reason that all ignored the issue of "general liquidity" and regarded the money supply an exogenous entity subject to control by means of nonqualitative open market operations. From an original reliance on the deliberate use of interest rates to affect the demand for credit via changes in the cost of credit to borrowers, there was a shift in the 1950s to the supply-side doctrines of credit availability. We are back once more on the demand side. By the application of monetarist principles, interest rates in 1981 soared to such heights as to reactivate the "interest-incentive effect" on borrowers. Only this time the policy was not one of consciously manipulating interest rates. We lost control for a variety of reasons and the net result was the mass unemployment of the early 1980s.

A strong case can be made for returning to the major concern of Keynes in his *Tract on Monetary Reform*—the offsetting and control of changes in velocity, and to Myrdal's original recognition of the endogeneity of the money supply. As endogenous as the money supply may be, it does not mean that accommodation to the "needs of trade" takes place smoothly or equitably, or even fully, or that it is without cost in terms of distortions in the flow of credit. The problem of controlling the paths it takes by controlling the flow of credit through the economy remains—*a problem most Post Keynesian monetary theorists have ignored*. Post Keynesian theory must therefore move in the direction of combining selective credit controls with a permanent incomes policy. Not only must wages be controlled, but the flow of credit as well.

If Post Keynesian economics is to avoid degenerating to tinkering with mechanical solutions, it must move in the direction of economic planning within a capitalist system that entails a social contract for the distribution of income—to be worked out jointly by capital, labor, and government. It must also require the "socialization of investment" that Keynes discussed toward the end of his *General Theory*. The problem is clearly defined by A. C. Pigou:

> [I]nvestment whether carried out by the State itself or under the influence
> of State bounties, if it were undertaken in fields where private investors
> were accustomed to operate, would entail a falling-off of investment by
> them; and this reaction *might* be carried so far that aggregate investment
> was hardly increased at all . . . Plainly, however, in an economy where
> State investment normally constitutes a large part of the whole, this
> difficulty will be comparatively unimportant.[16]

The direct socialization of investment, however, need not imply massive amounts of state investment. The same effect could be achieved
through direct and selective controls over the flow of private credit in
the economy. However it is to be done, Pigou is clear about the *financing* of such investment.

> It must be understood . . . that State action of this character, if it is
> financed by taking in taxes money that private persons would otherwise
> have themselves devoted either to investment or to the purchase of con-
> sumption goods, will not accomplish its purpose. *It must be accompanied
> by the creation of new money, mainly in the form of bank credit.* (Pp. 58–
> 59, italics supplied)

And, it should be stressed, with a selective control over the flow of this
increased supply of credit in keeping with the government's planning
objectives.

Some second thoughts

The combination of an *incomes policy* with *selective credit controls* is
not meant and cannot serve as a cure-all for the ills and troubles of a
capitalist society. The path of capitalism through historical time will
continue to be problematical and its survival in the very long run cannot
be assured. The need for a willful coordination of economic policy is a
recognition that the allocation of resources through an impersonal
market system is nothing more than the stuff and mythology of economic textbooks. The unavoidable alternative is the discretionary application of human intelligence to the solution of social problems. If a
permanent incomes policy and a system of selective credit controls
prove to be politically impossible, as they well might be either singly or
in combination, then *that* is the problem of capitalism.

As for the theory itself, American Post Keynesian economics seeks
to make capitalism, in revised form, a more workable and viable

enterprise, while ignoring some rather fundamental problems associated with contemporary capitalism. The source of capitalism's instability is not rooted exclusively in uncertainty and the problems associated with a credit-money economy (which have been the main preoccupations of American Post Keynesian economics); it is also to be found in the struggle over the division of the surplus between capital and labor. The resolution of economic problems in a capitalist society therefore requires a fundamental restructuring of political and economic power. Short-term solutions to the problem of inflation such as a tax-based incomes policy and selective credit controls, even if feasible, would not of themselves necessarily solve the problem of accumulation and long-term growth, though to the extent they brought the problem within politically tolerable limits they would buttress the legitimacy of the system by depoliticizing the distribution of the social product.

In essence, that was what Keynes sought to do in the *General Theory*. Though the founder of a revolution in economic thought, he was not, politically, a revolutionary. His main objective was to rid the system of its excesses and in doing so to assure its continuation. The tradegy is that Keynes's "revolution" was quickly captured and declawed. Although Post Keynesians are more in agreement in their rejection of "bastard" Keynesianism than they are among themselves, their common purpose is to restore Keynes's basic vision and to adapt it to a changed capitalism half a century after the publication of the *General Theory*.

Notes

1. *Principal Memoranda of Evidence*, p. 49.
2. Radcliffe Committee *Report*, p. 133, italics supplied.
3. For Keynes's earlier and even then prescient views, see Chapter 3, Part I of his *Tract on Monetary Reform* (London: Macmillan, 1923). For an evaluation, see Rousseas, *Monetary Theory*, pp. 42–48.
4. R. S. Sayers, *Modern Banking*, 6th ed. (London: Oxford University Press, 1964), italics supplied.
5. Ibid. See pp. 127–129 for Sayers' argument on moral suasion.
6. Cf. R. C. Lewontin, "Darwin's Revolution," *New York Review of Books*, June 16, 1983.
7. See Chapter 5 above.
8. E. A. Goldenweiser, *American Monetary Policy* (New York: McGraw-Hill, 1951), pp. 32–63.
9. Alarums will no doubt be raised on the dangers of monetizing the public debt, but such monetization need not take place. Control over credit volume would still be maintained selectively in keeping with the policy objectives of the government. As it is, even under current arrangements, the banking system and the central bank must, one

way or another, accommodate the financing needs of the government over and above what the public chooses to hold. The question is, at what price and, given the extraordinary heights of recent interest rates, with what effect on the distribution of income? Admittedly, cost pressure would be mitigated for the government, but such pressure has not really ever impeded a government from raising the monies it felt it had to have—witness the financing of the annual deficits of over $200 billion of the Reagan administration. Irresponsible governments are unlikely to be inhibited by the cost of the public debt. And irresponsible or not, the market argument of inefficient resource allocation cannot be taken seriously in an economy that is saturated with unequal concentrations of market power to begin with.

10. Goldenweiser, *American Monetary Policy*, p. 53, italics supplied.

11. It should be recalled that under the original Federal Reserve Act of 1913, the Secretary of the Treasury was the chairman of the Federal Reserve Board, which also included the Comptroller of the Currency—both in an *ex officio* capacity. It was not until the Banking Act of 1935 that the board was reconstituted in its present form.

12. The standard references are: Paul Davidson, *Money and the Real World*, 2nd ed., (New York: Macmillan, 1978); Paul Davidson and J. A. Kregel, "Keynes's Paradigm: A Theoretical Framework for Monetary Analysis," in Edward J. Nell, ed., *Growth, Profits and Property* (New York: Cambridge University Press, 1980); and Hyman P. Minsky, *Can "It" Happen Again?* (Armonk, N. Y.: M. E. Sharpe, Inc., 1982).

13. For an alternate view, see Stephen Rousseas, *Capitalism and Catastrophe* (New York: Cambridge University Press, 1978).

14. It can be argued that monetarism uses the same basic framework as "bastard" Keynesianism and that Milton Friedman is simply the most extreme example of a neoclassical Keynesian.

15. Kaldor, *Scourge* p. 18, italics supplied.

16. A. C. Pigou, *Keynes' General Theory: A Restrospect* (London: Macmillan, 1950), p. 58, original italics.

Bibliography

Committee on the Working of the Monetary System: Principal Memoranda of Evidence, Vol. 3, Part XIII. London: Her Majesty's Stationery Office, 1959.

Committee on the Working of the Monetary System: [Radcliffe] *Report*. London: Her Majesty's Stationery Office, August 1959.

Davidson, Paul. *Money and the Real World*, 2nd ed. New York: Macmillan, 1978.

———. "Why Money Matters." *Journal of Post Keynesian Economics*, Fall 1978.

Davidson, Paul, and Kregel, J. A., "Keynes's Paradigm: A Theoretical Framework for Monetary Analysis," in *Growth, Profits and Property*, ed. by Edward J. Nell. New York: Cambridge University Press, 1980.

Eichner, Alfred S., ed. *A Guide to Post Keynesian Economics*, Armonk, N. Y.: M. E. Sharpe, Inc. 1979.

Fayerabend, Paul. *Against Method*. New Jersey: Humanities Press, 1975.

Forman, Leonard; Groves, Miles; and Eichner, Alfred S. "The Demand Curve for Money Further Considered." In *Money and Macro Policy*, ed. by Marc Jarsulic. Boston: Kluwer-Nijhoff, 1984.

Garvy, George, and Blyn, Martin R. *The Velocity of Money*. New York: Federal Reserve Bank of New York, 1969.

Goldenweiser, E. A. *American Monetary Policy*. New York: McGraw-Hill, 1951.

Jarsulic, Marc. ed. *Money and Macro Policy*. Boston: Kluwer-Nijhoff, 1984.

Kaldor, Nicholas. "The New Monetarism." *Lloyds Bank Review*, July 1970.

———. *Origins of the New Monetarism*. Cardiff: University College Cardiff Press, 1980.

———. *The Scourge of Monetarism*. London: Oxford University Press, 1982.

Kalecki, Michal. *Selected Essays on the Dynamics of the Capitalist Economy, 1939–1970*. New York: Cambridge University Press, 1971.

Keynes, John Maynard. *The Economic Consequences of the Peace*. New York: Harcourt, Brace and Howe, 1920.

———. *A Tract on Monetary Reform*. London: Macmillan, 1923.

———. *A Treatise on Money*. London: Macmillan, 1930.

———. *The General Theory of Employment Interest and Money*. New York: Harcourt, Brace, 1936.

———. "The General Theory of Employment." *Quarterly Journal of Economics*, February 1937.

———. "Alternative Theories of the Rate of Interest." *Economic Journal*, June 1937.

———. "The 'Ex Ante' Theory of the Rate of Interest." *Economic Journal*, December 1937.

Kregel, J. A. "From Post-Keynes to Pre-Keynes." *Social Research*, Summer 1979.

Lavoie, Marc. "The Endogenous Flow of Credit and the Post Keynesian Theory of Money." Unpublished, May 1983.

———. "Credit and Money: The Dynamic Circuit, Overdraft Economics, and Post-Keynesian Economics." In *Money and Macro Policy*, ed. by Marc Jarsulic. Boston: Kluwer-Nijhoff, 1985.

Lekachman, Robert, ed. *Keynes' General Theory: Reports of Three Decades*. New York: St. Martin's Press, 1964.

Lichtenstein, Peter M. *An Introduction to Post-Keynesian and Marxian Theories of Value and Price*. Armonk, N. Y.: M. E. Sharpe, Inc. 1983.

Meek, Paul *U.S. Monetary Policy and Financial Markets*. New York: Federal Reserve Bank of New York, 1982.

Merleau-Ponti, Maurice. *Humanism and Terror*. Boston: Beacon Press, 1969; original French edition, 1947.

Minsky, Hyman P. "Central Banking and Money Market Changes." *Quarterly Journal of Economics*, May 1957.

———. *John Maynard Keynes*. New York: Columbia University Press, 1975.

———. *Can "It" Happen Again? Essays on Instability and Finance*, Armonk, N. Y.: M. E. Sharpe, Inc., 1982.

Moore, Basil. "The Endogenous Money Stock." *Journal of Post Keynesian Economics*, Fall 1979.

———. "Unpacking the Post Keynesian Black Box: Bank Lending and the Money Supply." *Journal of Post Keynesian Economics*, Summer 1983.

———. "Unpacking the Post Keynesian Black Box: Wages, Bank Lending and the Money Supply." *Thames Papers on Political Economy*, 1983.

———. "Keynes and the Endogeneity of the Money Supply." Unpublished, 1983.

———. "Wages, Bank Lending, and the Endogeneity of Credit Money." In *Money and Macro Policy*, ed. by Marc Jarsulic. Boston: Kluwer-Nijhoff, 1985.

Moore, B. J., and Stuttman, S. "A Causality Analysis of the Determinants of Money Growth." *British Review of Economic Issues*, Summer 1984.

Moore, B. J., and Threadgold, A. "Bank Lending and the Money Supply." *Bank of England Discussion Paper no. 10*, Boston, Bank of New England, July 1980.

Myrdal, Gunnar. *Monetary Equilibrium*. London: William Hodge & Co., Ltd., 1939.

Nell, Edward J., ed. *Growth, Profit and Property*. New York: Cambridge University Press, 1980.

Pasinetti, Luigi. *Growth and Income Distribution: Essays in Economic Theory*. London: Cambridge University Press, 1974.

Pigou, A. C., *Keynes' General Theory: A Retrospect*. London: Macmillan, 1950.

Principal Memoranda of Evidence. See *Committee on the Working of the Monetary System: Principal Memoranda of Evidence*.

Radcliffe Committee Report. See *Committee on the Working of the Monetary System: Report*.

Reynolds, Peter J. "Kalecki's Degree of Monopoly." *Journal of Post Keynesian Economics*, Spring 1983.

Robinson, Joan, and Wilkinson, F. "Employment Policy." *Cambridge Journal of Economics*, March 1977.

Rousseas, Stephen. "Velocity Changes and the Effectiveness of Monetary Policy, 1951–57." *Review of Economics and Statistics*, February 1960.

———. *Monetary Theory*. New York: Random House, 1972.

———. *Capitalism and Catastrophe*. New York: Cambridge University Press, 1978.

———. *The Political Economy of Reaganomics: A Critique*. Armonk, N. Y.: M. E. Sharpe, Inc. 1982.

Roncaglia, Alessandro. *Sraffa and the Theory of Prices*. Chichester: John Wiley & Sons, 1978.

Samuelson, Paul. "The General Theory," *Econometrica*, July 1946. Reprinted in Robert Lekachman, ed. *Keynes' General Theory: Reports of Three Decades*. New York: St. Martin's Press, 1964.

Sayers, R. S. *Modern Banking*, 6th ed. London: Oxford University Press, 1964.

Shackle, G. L. S. *The Years of High Theory*. London: Cambridge University Press, 1967.

Solomon, Anthony M. "Financial Innovation and Monetary Policy." New York: Federal Reserve Bank of New York, 1982.

Sraffa, Piero. *The Production of Commodities by Means of Commodities*. London: Cambridge University Press, 1960.

Weintraub, Sidney. *Keynes, Keynesians, and Monetarists*. Philadelphia: University of Pennsylvania Press, 1978.

———. *Capitalism's Inflation and Unemployment Crisis*. Reading, Mass.: Addison-Wesley, 1978.

Index